Justine Allain-Chapman has
Diocese of Southwark, as both
Principal of the South East Ins
course which trains a large num

**New Library of Pastoral Care**

# Resilient Pastors

*The role of adversity
in healing and growth*

Justine Allain-Chapman

First published in Great Britain in 2012

Society for Promoting Christian Knowledge
36 Causton Street
London SW1P 4ST
www.spckpublishing.co.uk

*British Library Cataloguing-in-Publication Data*
A catalogue record for this book is available from the British Library

ISBN 978–0–281–06383–3
eBook ISBN 978–0–281–06901–9

Typeset by Caroline Waldron, Wirral, Cheshire
First printed in Great Britain by MPG Books
Subsequently digitally printed in Great Britain

Produced on paper from sustainable forests

# Contents

*For Thomas*

# Acknowledgements

This book, and the doctoral research which has informed it, could not have been undertaken without financial support and I wish to express my thanks to all those people who have made decisions that have enabled me to undertake this research. Support has been given by the South East Institute for Theological Education, the Diocese of Rochester, the Isabella Gilmore Fund administered by the Diocese of Southwark, King's College London Theological Trust, the Women's Continuing Ministerial Education Trust administered by the Ministry Division of the Church of England, and the Verein der Freunde des IFZ, the Resilience Project, Munich.

I was privileged to be able to take a sabbatical and am grateful to the Makhad Trust for a retreat in the Egyptian desert in February 2010 and the opportunity to study at the International Research Centre of the Resilience Project linked to the University of Salzburg in February and March 2010. Most particularly, I am grateful to its director, Clemens Sedmak, who is also the F. D. Maurice Professor of Moral and Social Theology in the Department of Theology and Religious Studies at King's College London and was my doctoral supervisor. His support, challenge and uncanny ability to remember the publication dates of books and articles have been invaluable in shaping this work.

This research has been inspired by those many Christians, friends, parishioners, colleagues and students whose adversity I have witnessed and whose struggles I have shared, and whose lives of faith, hope and love have shaped and strengthened me as a person, as a Christian disciple and as a priest. I express my deepest gratitude to my husband Thomas who has been a source of strength for many years and who, along with our four children, enables me to face the struggles of life by love, singing and humour.

# CHAPTER ONE

# The need for resilience in pastoral ministry

## RESILIENT PASTORS

I have been fortunate enough to come across quite a few resilient pastors in my life. They have been people who have somehow been able to convey to me some strength and insight, sometimes by only the briefest encounter, that has enabled me to continue with a touch more courage and fortitude when life has been difficult. Resilient pastors are those who are able to feel and convey their sadness about a situation and show compassion. Such compassion often involves facing a difficult truth and naming it, and yet conveying it in a way that is as gentle or as firm as is necessary to help another see it. A good pastor addresses you in your situation, without glib phrases or pat answers. Able to share in the joy and sorrow of others, good pastors have the wisdom and maturity to lay down burdens for times of rest and renewal. Good pastors are resilient. They continue to grow in wisdom and compassion through the struggles of their own lives and in the difficulties they encounter in their ministry.

No doubt you will easily be able to identify people you could describe as resilient, those whom adversity has somehow strengthened. It is not that these people do not struggle, but they are not bitter and twisted by the experiences of life; instead, they are more open and loving. Some of these people may be pastors, involved formally in caring for others in Christian communities; others may show their care in informal roles. I expect you can also identify people who have a role of pastoral care, but don't seem very pastoral. They may seem unable either to feel or to express compassion towards those in adversity, or, at the other extreme, they are completely overwhelmed by the needs of others. You may recognize the possibility of these tendencies in yourself at times.

## THE PERSONAL EXPERIENCE OF BEING A PASTOR

I have presented pastors as people with particular qualities, and resilient pastors as those who have these qualities because they have come through difficult experiences well and thus developed empathy and compassion. Pastors do need to be approachable. They need to be able to convey that they are there to help. They also need to know how they can help, how to enable people experiencing adversity to come through it well, and be able to guide congregations who want to offer pastoral care to one another and want to know how to help rather than hinder.

This book is aimed at ordained or lay people who want to know how to help others and themselves be strengthened by the difficulties of life. It is particularly for those who live their lives in the context of Christian discipleship and ministry – not because it gives lots of helpful hints for churches, but because it draws on the stories and themes of Christian theology. However, I hope much of it will also be of value to those who do not seek to draw on Christian faith explicitly, but seek both a coherent understanding of what enables people to be strengthened in adversity and resources to nourish themselves as well as others. I have sought to provide a way of understanding the dynamics of adversity so as to give shape and direction to the experience. I do this by drawing on contemporary research into resilience, and on the Christian tradition in the past and also in the present where the insights of psychology can be included. I have written to help people make sense of the personal costs of pastoral care, costs that in some strange way bring about satisfaction and fulfilment. I hope that what I write will provide a resource to all those who, inevitably, will at some point in their lives face adversity. But it will particularly be a resource for pastors by providing the pointers so that they recognize the dynamics of developing resilience for themselves, as well as enabling strengthening in others.

I have sought to provide a shape and direction to the task of how to help people be strengthened in adversity. I have also sought to provide a theological understanding of what the pastor goes through in witnessing adversity and having the responsibility of trying to help. Not surprisingly, my motivation for trying to do this comes out of my experience, as a person and as a pastor, of finding that although Christians are keen to help people who are in difficulties of any kind, from formal chaplaincy work such as in hospitals and prisons to visiting someone at home, there is little consensus about what will help people come through large and small difficulties well. There is also very little sense about how what we preach and teach in churches prepares people for the difficulties of life or helps them grow through them.

## DOES FAITH MAKE ANY DIFFERENCE?

As I have reflected on my personal experience as a priest in the Church of England, I have seen that my own formation and growth as a pastor have been shaped by three periods of my life where I have had questions about how, or indeed whether, faith helps people in adversity.

### Formation as a child

When I was ten years old, my mother was diagnosed with cancer with which she struggled for several years before recovering and going on to live for many more decades. It was at this time that my call to be a pastor was forged as I saw what my mother went through, found a new depth of faith, and witnessed the pastoral care offered by the church. My mother's experience, typically, was of battling with cancer, of a fight to survive and of treatments as harsh as the disease itself. The prayers for her recovery offered and promised by other people meant a great deal to her, as did cards, visits and practical help. My mother was devastated when a friend crossed over to the other side of the street when she saw her, because, as she explained to my mother later, she did not know what to say. When my mother met ministers in the hospital or when they visited at home she would comment on whether they prayed with her: she was less interested in expensive flowers and in more need of someone with whom she could both express her fears and be helped to take them to God in faith. That said, she found the ironing taken away and returned by a devout Christian friend of more use than the biblical commentaries that the same friend brought round for her sustenance. It was very clear to me that for my mother to win this struggle and come through, she needed to believe that her life was worth it, and she needed others to show appropriate support for her, emotional, practical and spiritual.

In this first phase of formation as a Christian and as a pastor I had believed that Christian faith should make a difference to facing and enduring adversity, but discovered that it hadn't done so, or not as I had expected it would. I had seen that honest acknowledgement and sharing of the struggle were a more significant component of spiritual support than conveying propositional truth. Supportive relationships, I could see, helped my mother, and enabled her to carry on in her darkest times.

## Formation as a new pastor

Pastoral work as a curate was the second period of pastoral formation in my life and a baptism by fire for me, since my first couple of years of ordained ministry included the full range of traumatic pastoral situations within the congregation. These situations included suicide, stillbirth, death by accident and cancer. I began to develop an interest in pastoral ministry around death, dying and bereavement. I expected that by being ordained I should have answers, be able to provide for people experiencing adversity, and be able to do some good; I believed that prayer would somehow help and, failing that, love would. It seemed that other people had similar expectations as to what I should be able to provide for them. Those who did not profess Christian faith seemed to think that because I had faith I would not be too affected by such things as personal bereavement.

My role meant that I saw the intimacies of physical pain and death, heard the screams, witnessed the tears, and yet had to hold myself together, observe confidentiality, and could often feel very alone at the funeral tea. I was not the one bereaved, was I? And yet I still felt grief. As a new pastor I experienced being overwhelmed by witnessing such suffering, and also found that suffering resonating with me so that I felt pain that somehow was – and yet wasn't – mine. I realized I had 'stuff' and pastoring people in adversity gave my pain an outlet as well as swamping and draining me.

In the congregation I found people who were full of faith, people who had experienced, been broken by and then strengthened through, suffering. They were people who were able to express their despair, anxiety, fear and vulnerability in ways that certainly gave me a language of suffering and of faith within it. The prayer groups and meditations led by such Christians had a quality of honesty and not traditional piety. I also, of course, encountered those for whom faith seemed to be packaged or held in such a way that they told me that God provided them with instant peace and trust. There were others for whom the fact that they were churchgoers did not lead them to call on the church or its pastoral resources to help them when adversity struck because – either by expectation or experience – they didn't believe it would help.

I was challenged to consider whether what I had been taught as a Christian, and what I was preaching and teaching then, prepared people to be resilient in the face of adversity or inhibited their ability to come through well. Was the usual perspective conveyed at Christmas and Easter, for example, an invitation to accept God's will and trust him passively, exemplified by Mary's obedience and Jesus' silence when accused and his acceptance of death? Were the words of the blessing about the peace of God that passes all understanding received as a burden on people experiencing difficulty because they thought they should feel calm rather than struggle? Such perspectives did not ring true with the visceral faith of those around me, honestly struggling and full of faith and life, even in the face of death.

In this second period of pastoral formation, I saw that Christian faith and community – where there was honest acknowledgement of the struggle and supportive relationships – did form people who were resilient. They suffered and came through, wiser, more loving, more real. The suffering was real, however, and the cost to me was profound.

## Forming others

My third period of experience and reflection on pastoring those who might well be strengthened by their adversity is in teaching pastoral care dimensions of Practical Theology to those training for ministry. Here, among the variety of models of ministry and pastoral care, the model of the 'wounded healer' has a significant place. In teaching pastoral care I see that this model appeals to those in particular who have experienced adversity as something that has brought them to faith. It appeals less to those who believe that they are called to provide comfort and healing, for whom proclaiming God's Word takes priority. In overseeing pastoral placements in prisons, hospitals and hospices I see students encounter similar issues to those I did as a new pastor – the overwhelming scale and nature of human suffering that prevents a quick 'Jesus is the answer' approach to pastoral care and requires a strategy and understanding of what can help. I observe that witnessing other people's pain resonates with their own personal history. As it comes to the surface, they need to make sense of it and grow in faith through it.

# THE NEED FOR A PASTORAL THEOLOGY OF RESILIENCE

My experience as a pastor and as a theological educator leads me to seek a pastoral theology of resilience which gives a theological understanding of being strengthened in adversity, revisits the model of the wounded healer, and provides strategies and resources for the pastor that not only work, but take account of the person of the pastor as well as those whom he or she pastors.

I realized that I needed to research how Christians, and particularly pastors, can help people experiencing adversity to be strengthened. I also wanted to find out how pastors can be strengthened as they exercise a ministry of pastoral care. The exploration of these two questions will enable me to develop a pastoral theology of resilience which pastors can draw on both to enable resilience in others and for themselves in order to be resilient pastors.

Part of the reason that the questions I am asking have emerged now is due to the trend in society which encourages people to think for themselves and not take what is said by authority figures at face value. Clergy have become more aware of inadequacies in pastoral care and teaching and are confronted personally by suffering and direct questions about where God is. Clergy have lost status, but gained access to the everyday experiences and problems of people, who no longer hide their personal issues and questions behind their 'best Christian face'.[1] A re-evaluation of theology related to being strengthened in adversity and caring for those experiencing adversity has become necessary for new understanding to emerge and effect change in teaching and in the practice of pastoral care.

These questions, arising as they do out of the experience of pastoral ministry, fall into the theological discipline of Practical or Pastoral Theology. Practical or Pastoral Theology is the area of theological study that seeks to draw on many aspects of human and theological knowledge in order to come to conclusions which will shape and reshape the understanding and practice of Christian discipleship and ministry. Quite how to integrate the strands has been the subject of discussion and has led to practical and pastoral theologians putting forward a variety of methodological models. There is considerable disagreement about the approaches and methods of Practical or Pastoral Theology, with the tension surrounding the relative importance given to theology, contemporary experience and non-theological disciplines. Critique of methods of theological reflection generally focuses on the weakness in the use of traditional sources, particularly the Bible, so that analysis of local contexts and socio-economic factors emerges as more accomplished than engagement with it or with Christian history and doctrine.

Practical theologians have identified a variety of models of theological reflection by which human experience can take its place and the critique of Christian practices and teaching come into conversation not only with the traditional disciplines of theology, but in order to effect change. The most well-known model of theological reflection is the pastoral cycle, which attempts to overcome the rationalist distinction between theory and practice and enable theology to use the human or social sciences in an integrated way, so that it reflects on Christian theology and Christian practice and leads to action, or praxis. The pastoral cycle or praxis model comes out of the Marxist tradition and the educational philosophy of Paulo Freire, and it employs a hermeneutic of suspicion with regard to Christian theology and practice. The best-known example of the use of this methodology is drawn from Liberation Theology and the base communities of Latin America, where the Bible and the sacraments became an inspiration for and a means to a critical understanding of the social and political situation.

## CONVERSATION FOR A PASTORAL THEOLOGY OF RESILIENCE

The correlation or analogical or dialogical model of theological reflection sets up a conversation well suited as an approach to address the questions of how Christians, and particularly pastors, can help people experiencing adversity to be strengthened, and how pastors can be strengthened as they exercise a ministry of pastoral care. The conversation model seeks to honour and balance the heritage of the gospel and the contemporary situation by creating a developing dialectic made up of conversation partners who bring a range of resources. The practical theologian Stephen Pattison proposes and explores the term and method of *critical conversation*. It is the approach that I will use throughout this book, because there are various strands of human and Christian knowing and experience to listen to in order to consider how to help people be strengthened in adversity. Each chapter will introduce a conversation partner and our understanding will build so that our pastoral practice can be enriched.

Conversation as a model has many strengths:

- Conversation lies at the centre of human and pastoral encounters.
- Conversation works with the hiddenness of human personality, thus pointing to the need to express theology in terms of story, myth, metaphor, image and symbol.
- Conversations take into account more than the propositional, rational and logical.
- Conversations do not necessarily proceed in a straightforward

direction or at the same level. A willingness to attend, listen and
learn is presupposed, as is the expectation of transformation.

- Conversation in this model of theological reflection is three-
  way: between one's own ideas, beliefs, feelings, perceptions and
  assumptions; the beliefs, assumptions and perceptions provided
  by the Christian tradition; and the contemporary situation that
  is being examined.
- Conversations evolve, function at different levels, allow for different starting points to be identified.
- In conversation partners show a willingness to listen so that
  the participants are changed, and end up seeing themselves and
  others from a new angle.[2]

A conversation about how best to help other people and be a
good pastor isn't new, of course. It is not unreasonable to expect
that the literature of pastoral care has already addressed the area
of being strengthened in adversity as Christians and as pastors,
and what has been written has shaped the direction of this book.
Pastoral care, however, is no longer at the cutting-edge of Practical Theology as it was in the 1980s. This is related to an emphasis on mission, leadership and management in church life, which
has come to the fore so that pastoral care has been relegated.
There is a gap and a need to attend to the practice of pastoral care.
Research into the reasons why people leave church include being
let down by the church, particularly the clergy, and a feeling that
the pastoral care has been unprofessional. Of those under 40, 14
per cent of church leavers felt that the church had let them down
when they needed support; the figure for those over 40 was 21 per
cent. These people, most of whom were female, blamed the clergy
for not providing sufficient care. Francis and Richter point out that
their research suggests that people have too high expectations of
the clergy and clergy have too high expectations of themselves.
Mechanisms are clearly needed to help clergy deal with their emotions when church leavers let them know that they are blaming
clergy for their disengagement with church life, as well as regular
disciplined review of individual practice. With 4 per cent of church
leavers feeling psychologically abused and 1 per cent having been
sexually abused, attention to the abuse of power also needs to be

given in the selection, training and supervision of pastors.[3] There is a need for pastors to develop resilience and to do so by understanding and practising how this can happen.

Clearly, pastoral care is important and it is vital that it is done well. One of the criticisms of pastoral care is that it neglects the Bible, another that it focuses too much on skills. These criticisms have guided the choice of my conversation partners so that we will engage with the Bible through story, but predominantly through metaphor, as well as drawing on the pithy sayings of the desert elders.

The criticism that the pastoral care literature has prioritized pastoral skills, such as counselling and listening skills, rather than drawing on the resources of the Christian tradition has been taken up in recent years by a development of an understanding and practice of pastoral supervision.[4] Writing on pastoral supervision addresses the nature of the pastoral relationship as well as the learning relationship between a pastor and a supervisor. Being supervised is not only important when you are training to be a pastor or minister, but throughout ministry as an aspect of theologically reflecting on ministry. Ward develops a model of supervision that focuses on the quality of the relationship, rejecting metaphors associated with the term 'oversight' for their lack of recognition of involvement. She explores the hierarchical connotations and recognizes the costly, though potentially mutually enriching, nature of the relationship.[5] Questions too are being asked about whether the methods drawn from counselling or those of spiritual direction might be most appropriate in the supervision of ministers. I will attend to the debate and concerns that relate to the place of counselling skills and pastoral supervision in pastoral care by a reinterpretation of the model of the wounded healer as well as by drawing on the relationship of desert elder to disciple.

## CONVERSATION PARTNERS

The conversation partners I use have been chosen to answer my questions about how Christians, and particularly pastors, can help people experiencing adversity to be strengthened, and how pastors can be strengthened as they exercise a ministry of pastoral care. The conversation partners chosen mean that we can draw insight from

- the human sciences through studies in resilience;
- the biblical, spiritual and theological tradition through the desert experience in the Bible, texts of the desert Christians and the theology of Rowan Williams;
- the reflections of pastoral theologians through literature of the myth and pastoral care model of the wounded healer.

In Chapter 2 the multidisciplinary psychosocial science research into resilience explores contemporary research on the human experience of being strengthened in adversity, and quite naturally forms the first conversation partner. Pastoral literature has not engaged with the concept of resilience or the body of literature devoted to it. Resilience literature is wide in scope, identifying many factors as contributing to the resilience of individuals, families and communities. Factors which can be influenced by the work of the pastor and emerge from the literature focus on struggle, the self and relationships. These three factors are essential to building resilience and present challenges to Christian theology as well as to the practice of pastoral care. I have discovered that resilience literature identifies a process of resilience that begins in adversity and leads to altruism, and in doing so sheds light on the life stories and experience of pastors.

Having drawn from resilience literature the themes of struggle, self and relationships and observed the direction of growth from adversity to altruism, I turn in Chapter 3 to the Bible as an essential conversation partner. The theme of the desert emerged as one that resonated with the experience of struggle and a strengthening out of which comes the ministry of pastoral leadership. Using the desert as a motif appeals to the human propensity for the religious and symbolic and goes some way to enabling pastoral theology to be transformational. The desert motif echoes with other pastoral, spiritual and ministerial literature. Its appeal in contemporary thought is therefore wide enough for it to resonate with human experience and also to point people towards the Bible and Christian history. Belden Lane, for example, explores dying and bereavement against the backdrop of fierce landscapes in a book which addresses pastoral care and spirituality. Henri Nouwen uses the motif of desert to explore contemporary ministry, as does Christopher Moody in using the motif of wilderness.[6]

The desert metaphor provides an important way to engage pastors and ordinands for whom rooting Christian practice in the Bible is primary, and can draw on the insights of the human sciences and Christian theology, past and present, by engagement with the desert motif. By exploring contemporary scholarship of the desert narratives of Moses and Hagar, traditional interpretations of the narratives are revealed and can be challenged. This echoes the challenges of resilience literature to pastoral care, particularly around the themes of obedience and autonomy. It also challenges the priority of Liberation Theology and affirms the place of endurance which seeks survival by struggle and quality of life.

The motif and narratives of the desert explored in this research provide a vision for enabling people to be resilient. This is apt in the current climate of pastoral care offered towards many who are not Christians, for example at the pastoral offices of weddings and funerals as well as in sector ministries such as hospital and prison chaplaincies. The motif is evocative of adversity and, once explored, takes someone suffering on a path to being strengthened by the experience. This can be so for those who espouse no religious faith, as well as people of non-Christian faiths where narratives resonate because the desert is a place of adversity and encounter which enables growth. This research uses Old Testament narratives shared by Christianity, Judaism and Islam, and builds on them in later chapters by recourse to texts of the desert Christians of the fourth and fifth centuries as well as to more recent Christian writing on desert spirituality to provide a Christian vision. Desert is a universal motif that can be used by lay pastors as well as clergy, with the Hagar narrative in particular providing a resource for women.

The conversation partner in Chapter 4 is the world of the desert Christians of the fourth and fifth centuries, read through the *Alphabetical Sayings*. These attend in particular to the need to embrace the desert as a refuge or as a place of adversity to which you go in order to grow.

In Chapter 5 the *Institutes* and *Conferences* of John Cassian provide an understanding of adversity in Christian life; it becomes a programme of growth which can begin in adversity and ends up beyond altruism and pastoral responsibility. Cassian's programme for growth promotes virtues such as obedience and humility which, on the face of it, are challenged by resilience literature as undermining people's ability to be strengthened in adversity.

Thus a conversation partner is needed in order to reinterpret something of the desert tradition for contemporary Christian theology. A resilience reading of the theology of Rowan Williams, in Chapter 6, provides a conversation with contemporary Christian theology as it addresses the themes of self, struggle and relationships in a way that is faithful to the tradition and yet appropriate to contemporary human experience and concerns. His use of the metaphors of speech and space resonate with the experience of the desert as landscape and metaphor.

Having focused primarily on the initial question of how Christians can help people experiencing adversity to be strengthened, a conversation in Chapter 7 with contemporary psychological as well as Christian understandings of the myth and model of the wounded healer addresses how pastors can be strengthened as they exercise a ministry of pastoral care. While the ancient myths describe a journey from adversity to altruism in the healer, pastoral care literature focuses on the model of the wounded healer in a positive way. The contemporary psychological literature, however, issues warnings of the danger of unhealed wounders. This raises the importance of self-awareness and a commitment to growth in the pastor, because a disregarding of their own woundedness and history of adversity undermines the ministry of pastoral care. As studies in resilience attest, there is a process of strengthening which begins in adversity and is expressed in altruism.

In drawing together these conversation partners I propose a pastoral theology of resilience with implications for teaching and preaching as well as for pastoral relationships. These will attend to helping people not only to be strengthened while in adversity, but also to prepare for adversity, and to find healing from adversity in the past.

# CHAPTER TWO

# Developing resilience: research and themes

## A CONVERSATION WITH STUDIES IN RESILIENCE

An obvious starting point for exploring the question of how to help people experiencing adversity to be strengthened is the empirical research into resilience. This looks at the study of why and how people have coped with and come through adversity strengthened.

Firmly placed in the movement for positive psychology, resilience literature affirms the possibility of coming through adversity well. The perspective of the literature is the study of strength and virtue, affirming the possibility of coming through adversity constructively, rather than focusing on pathology, weakness and damage. This, of course, is surely the experience and hope of Christian pastoral care which seeks to enable such a process of strengthening. That studies in resilience recognize the importance of the spiritual and religious in facilitating strengthening enables any conversation with the body of literature to be productive and insightful.

We need not expect that the findings of resilience literature will be unrecognizable to good pastors, but rather hope that such findings might provide focus and direction for giving an account of the place of adversity in human life and Christian faith as well as in caring for those experiencing adversity. Such focus and direction is needed by pastors for a range of aspects of pastoral ministry such as preaching or training a pastoral team. A conversation with resilience literature will enable foundations for a pastoral theology of resilience to be laid which will enable pastors to help those in adversity be strengthened. It will also bring insight regarding the ways in which pastors might cope and be strengthened personally in their pastoral ministry. We shall discover that there are three themes that studies in resilience reveal as particularly pertinent for pastoral care: struggle, self, and relationships. We shall also explore the insights that come from understanding the processes by which the resilient become altruistic and report experiencing healing through acts of compassion.

## INTRODUCING RESILIENCE

Resilience is defined as the capacity to bounce back. In physics the term resilience is used to refer to a material's quality to resist deformation or destruction and indeed to be strengthened by pressure or heating. The physical definition has obvious metaphorical parallels when considering the capacity of human beings to bounce back or come through crisis, difficulty or trauma. Furthermore, the observation that difficulty can somehow strengthen human beings also draws from its analogy with physical resilience since a certain type of pressure, such as stretching or heating, has a 'steeling' effect on metal.

In psychology, resilience is the positive capacity developed by people who are open and motivated to change in the face of adversity. The research into resilience represents a shift from overemphasizing pathology in the past, to recognizing the strengths in human character. Psychological studies which after the Second World War focused on healing and repairing damage have more recently included studies in happiness, virtue, excellence and optimal human flourishing. To focus on resilience is to recognize adversity, but to focus on strength. The resilient take up the struggle of dealing with the circumstances of their lives in such a way as to be strengthened personally by their experience. Resilient people are those who (in three 'C's) have *Coped* with adversity, been *Constant* in resisting destruction, and been able to *Construct* a new sense of themselves and their lives.

## STUDIES IN RESILIENCE

The concept of resilience was developed in the 1970s in social scientific research to discover what factors enabled some human beings to survive and even flourish against seemingly impossible odds. The early research came out of the observation that there were children from difficult backgrounds who thrived rather than showed the signs of trauma expected of them. Thus research into resilience did not begin as a theoretical enterprise, but as one rooted in human experience. Rather than looking at the risk factors that led to psychosocial problems, the studies focused on identifying the strengths of individuals who had unexpectedly overcome the difficulties of their past. The foundational research project of resilience was begun in 1955 by Emmy Werner, who first described as resilient 72 of 200 at-risk children in her study of a total of 700 children in Kauai, Hawaii. These children, despite factors such as having mentally ill or alcoholic parents, did not exhibit the destructive behaviours of the majority of teenagers in those same circumstances. Werner and Smith reported the longitudinal findings of the community after studying its children for 30 years, and identified many differences that favoured the resilient group.[1]

The shortlist of the qualities of the resilient, gained from research in different forms and situations and including an identification of characteristics of child, family, relationships or the environment, has been remarkably stable over time. It includes characteristics to do with health, cognitive ability, secure relationships, self-regulation and self-direction, motivation and positive outlook on life, spiritual and/or religious systems of belief and meaning, as well as family, peer, school and cultural systems. The resilient children grew up to be adults who possessed greater social maturity, nurturance, empathy, sense of responsibility and independence.

Michael Rutter studied youth in inner-city London and on the Isle of Wight. He found that a quarter of the children were resilient even though they might have experienced many risk factors. Being born female, he discovered, was a basic advantage. Other key qualities he identified were an easy temperament, having a positive school climate, self-mastery, self-efficacy, planning skills and a warm, close, personal relationship with an adult. Poverty and substance abuse were listed as major risk factors while intelligence, positive coping strategies, internal locus of control, and a meaningful relationship were deemed protective for individuals.[2]

Perhaps the most surprising conclusion that arose from these studies was the ordinariness of resilience itself. The realization that lots of children are resilient overturned many of the negative assumptions and deficit models about children growing up under the threat of disadvantage and adversity. The greatest threats to wellbeing are those that compromise the natural protective systems of a human being. The areas in which the protective systems may be jeopardized include brain development and cognition, caregiver/child relationships, regulation of emotion and behaviour, and the motivation for learning and engaging in the environment. One significant finding has been the evidence that despite being disadvantaged in early years a surprising number of children do recover and develop healthily, both cognitively and physically. This has been demonstrated in children who have been adopted from institutions characterized by extreme deprivation, such as those in Romania, where catch-up by the age of four was remarkable. Thus the goals of resilience education now incorporate the promotion of competence as well as the prevention or amelioration of symptoms and problems. Although adversity during childhood does impact more greatly on a person than in later life, we have become much more open to the possibility of change in the direction of recovery and healing with appropriate intervention.

Two major approaches of resilience research have sought to discover and explain how people become resilient. The first can be described as variable focused. It uses statistics to test for linkages among measures of the degree of risk or adversity, outcome, and the potential qualities of an individual or environment that may function to compensate for or protect the individual from the negative consequences of risk or adversity. The second research approach is person focused and focuses on whole individuals. The most complex person-oriented models compare healthy with maladaptive pathways in lives, through time, to give special attention to the turning points in people's lives. Much of the discussion in resilience has drawn on these case studies and has revealed that opportunities and choices at crucial times in people's lives play an important role in the lives of resilient individuals. The resilient take action that has positive consequences for their lives, such as finding mentors, entering the armed forces, finding a new or deeper faith, marrying healthy partners, or leaving a deviant group.

It is clear that the concept of resilience goes beyond a collection of traits; research points to resilience being a process that builds over time. It can be described as an ongoing and developing fund of energy and skill that can be used in current struggles or the active process of self-righting. This emphasizes that people do more than merely get through difficult emotional experiences: resilience includes the skills, abilities, knowledge and insight that accumulate over time as people struggle to surmount adversity. So *resilience is a process of coping with adversity, change, or opportunity*, in such a way as to identify, fortify, and enrich resilient qualities in a person. Resilience recognizes that adversity affects people so that the response to adversity cannot be pretence at invulnerability or invincibility. Resilience necessitates change, change that strengthens.

Since the definitions of resilience extend beyond just recovery or bouncing back to encompass growth or adaptation through disruption, so the research provides something of an umbrella for many if not most psychological and educational theories. The literature on resilience is multidisciplinary. Even within psychosocial science, studies include research into genetics, personality, cognitive development and human relationships. In addition, resilience is used as a concept outside psychosocial science. It is being applied to systems such as families and schools as well as to individuals, and also to the multilevel dynamics in systems at behavioural and cellular levels, including such dynamics as gene–environment interaction, social interactions, and person–media interactions. The impact of major disasters has shown dramatically that human life is interdependent on the resilience of many other systems, including ecosystems, computer, emergency, health care and communication systems, so that there is much to learn about human resilience in many other fields. Resilience has become a very popular concept.

## RESILIENCE AND FAITH

Resilience research makes room for a consideration of the role of religion and faith and gives attention to the spiritual and the theological. This is possible because of the recognition that resiliency goes beyond a simple scrutiny of external behaviour and circumstances. It involves motivation and self-perception, for example, which are shaped by religion and spirituality for good or ill. Spiritual resilience can be described as the capacity, when faced with adversity, to cope using religious resources. This includes resisting the destruction of one's spiritual qualities, and constructing something positive in line with larger theological goals. Studies exploring spiritual resilience have not been confined to the kind of spirituality that is expressed and experienced in traditional religious practice; the spirituality studied encompasses interpersonal and societal interactions, relationship to self, and the ability to go beyond the limits of self-interest, one's own experience, and horizon of meaning. It also includes an openness to spirit, understood variously as God, the divine, energy, source of life, mystery and what is beyond understanding.

Theology itself has also used the concept of resilience to enrich its own understanding of the human person, though not by that name. The use of the concept of resilience has its roots in classical theology, with St Thomas Aquinas reinterpreting Aristotle's classical virtues in such a way that, as Craig Titus argues, they provide a Christian concept of resilience in the form of the virtue of fortitude.[3] Aquinas presents virtue as the foundation for Christian moral theology and sees a person's ultimate goal as complete flourishing or happiness, with flourishing as the primary goal of his moral acts. In Aquinas's scheme of moral and intellectual virtues, fortitude is one of the four cardinal virtues and a moral virtue.[4] Fortitude may be translated as strength, vigour or courage. The associated virtues of fortitude are magnanimity, magnificence, patience and perseverance, which bring balance and focus to human action. Its two acts are initiative-taking and endurance, with initiative-taking underlying magnanimity and magnificence and endurance lying behind patience and perseverance. Fortitude is the virtue that helps us manage our fear and our daring as a capacity to resist degradation and as a principle to act. It is the mean between fear and daring. The vices associated with it are presumption, biting off more than you can chew, and pusillanimity, small-souledness, or biting off less.

The psychosocial science insights into resilience can be compared with Aquinas's virtue theory in that they both address not only the reality of difficulty but the resourcefulness needed to overcome it. The virtue of fortitude reveals what studies in resilience also show us, that it is an acquired strength which demands that we act creatively in new situations that endanger us and cause us fear, using such strategies as self-efficacy and confidence.

## RESILIENCE THEMES FOR A PASTORAL THEOLOGY OF RESILIENCE

Three themes most obviously emerge from resilience literature as potential building blocks for a pastoral theology of resilience: *struggle*, *self* and *relationships*. No one can develop resiliency without engaging in the struggle with adversity. That strengthening is gained by struggle, rather than perhaps by passivity or acquiescence to fate or God, is important to explore for a pastoral theology of resilience. The significance of the sense of self in resilience literature – encompassing self-awareness, self-esteem, agency, an inner locus of control, an inner life and self-discipline – needs to be explored for pastoral theology, as does the importance of relationships. These three themes – struggle, self and relationships – emerge naturally from the multidisciplinary body of resilience literature.

Pastoral ministry can rarely change the environmental or health factors contributing to adversity. Factors that relate to a person's sense of self, however, such as self-worth and motivation, can be influenced by both pastoral practice and preaching and teaching. The pastoral relationship is one relationship that might be of support to someone in adversity, as may the wider relationships that can be forged in a Christian community. A conversation between pastoral care and resilience literature is new. Both share the aim of seeking to help to strengthen those in adversity, and the research around these three themes is significant in contributing to pastoral care in a Christian context.

## AN EXAMPLE OF RESILIENCE: VIKTOR FRANKL

The classic work on resilience, *Man's Search for Meaning*, by Viktor Frankl, exemplifies the themes of struggle, self and relationships that an individual has developed and which are most pertinent in resourcing a pastoral theology of resilience.

Frankl describes the struggle to stay alive and to retain what it meant to be human in Auschwitz during the Second World War. He shows the need to take up the struggle and to resist seeing oneself as less than human. To understand oneself as having worth and choice, and to be resourced by an inner life that can imagine a future, builds resilience. Frankl's experiences describe the importance of self-perception, motivation, choice and relationships in being able to cope, resist destruction and come through the experience not only alive, but strengthened.

Frankl's primary objective was sheer physical survival enabled by inner motivation. At the beginning he struck out of his mind the whole of his former life in order to accept the situation. There were, of course many physical struggles associated with the pain and hardship of camp life, but what Frankl points to is a connection between body and spirit where the inner life protects the physical life. He describes those in a concentration camp with a rich intellectual life as surviving better than would be expected from their physical condition, because they could retreat to a life of inner riches and spiritual freedom. Religious belief was part of this inner life and expressed in improvised services and prayers in the corner of a hut. Once motivation to survive was gone, however, and a prisoner had given up faith in the strength to carry on, it seldom returned and death quickly ensued.

At first, camp life involved the emotional pain of longing for home, and the distress of watching deaths and beatings. Later Frankl observed the distancing and protective blunting of feelings that enabled prisoners to cope, along with a sense of apathy and regression to a more primitive form of life focused on thinking about food – not just because of the need for sustenance but to know that the subhuman existence would cease. After liberation, grasping freedom and feeling emotion was a process to be relearned in order to belong to the world again.

Self-perception also enabled survival. Frankl describes suffering as completely filling the human mind and soul and diminishing the sense of self – whether the suffering be large or small. Struggling and winning against the image of the self reduced to animal life, treated as an object to be exterminated and of no value, was thus difficult. It was vital, though, not to lose the sense of being an individual with a mind, with inner freedom and personal value.

## FRANKL'S CHOICE

For Frankl, survival was made possible by finding meaning and being aware that such meaning was part of his inner life and ability to choose how to approach the circumstances of his life: 'The experiences of camp life show that man does have a choice of action.'[5] His ability to be resilient was located in the inner choice to view his incarceration as a trial, and was fuelled by an inner life fed by the vision of love. It was the exercise of spiritual freedom in the inner decision to choose his attitude to the camp guards which gave meaning and purpose to him, turning the camp into an inner trial rather than a place to vegetate. Having an aim in life and a sense of the future were vital. A prisoner was doomed once he lost his faith in the future. Frankl imagined giving lectures on the psychology of the concentration camp. He describes prisoners in a concentration camp in general as motivated to keep alive by the thought of family waiting at home and by a desire to save their friends. Frankl was motivated to stay alive by an image of his wife:

> Then I grasped the meaning of the greatest secret that human poetry and human thought and belief have to impart: The salvation of man is through love and in love. I understand how a man who has nothing left in this world still may know bliss, be it only for a brief moment, in the contemplation of his beloved. In a position of utter desolation, when man cannot express himself in positive action, when his only achievement may consist in enduring his sufferings in the right way – an honourable way – in such a position man can, through loving contemplation of the image he carries of his beloved, achieve fulfilment.[6]

Despite not knowing whether she was alive or dead, it was in contemplation of the beloved that Frankl describes Love as finding its deepest meaning in the inner life. Frankl replaced the forced imprisonment and the absence of relationships of love, respect and kindness that characterized life in a concentration camp with his own response involving inner change, choice and growth helped by drawing on a loving relationship in his inner life. Suffering, for Frankl, is a destiny to be borne, something that life expects of a person, something with meaning, the unique opportunity lying in the way the burden is borne.

Frankl's account of his experience of surviving a concentration camp well highlights the significance of the three resilience themes of struggle, self and relationships. The motivation to survive demanded the struggle to resist destructive relationships and self-perceptions. An inner life resourced by the experiences of loving relationships and self-perceptions of worth, which could contemplate a future, enabled the strength needed to survive.

Let us look at these themes as they emerge in studies in resilience with a view to considering their importance in shaping the direction of the practice of pastoral care and a pastoral theology of resilience.

## STRUGGLE

Resilience literature presents us with the findings that struggle hurts but is central to what it means to change and grow in the course of ordinary human life. To struggle involves using energy to get free of restriction or meet difficulty or opposition, energy which reveals signs of life. Struggle is necessary and it enables resilience. Where a person seeks to grow, struggle needs to be sought. Struggle is a religious theme, characterizing many of the lives of biblical characters and saints, and in the contemporary context it can have political, community and individual dimensions. The resilience literature considered in the context of pastoral care points to the centrality and vitality of struggle rather than a passive peace.

As a psychiatrist, Frederic Flach became convinced that struggle is necessary for change and for growth in human life. He describes ordinary human maturing as not easy: indeed, throughout the life cycle there are points such as puberty or retirement which are often accompanied by emotional pain. Struggle arises because of the emotional pain and loss of control that are associated with disruption in human life and experienced in both the body and the mind. To deny the pain or to medicate too quickly, Flach argues, prevents the person from enacting the change needed in order to grow. After years of clinical practice Flach came to see that personal struggle and falling apart are signs of strength which enable people to integrate their experiences and change attitudes and patterns of behaviour. Flach suggested that resilient qualities are attained through a law of disruption and reintegration, since times of change and disruption in human life are characterized by the demand to struggle, to adapt and overcome the difficulty presenting itself.

When people want to change and are motivated to personal growth, studies in resilience recommend activities involving struggle, planned disruptions which are solutions to stagnation so that people can seek to find meaning and purpose. A planned disruption will involve activities that put you under pressure, such as a diet or exercise regime. Giving something up for Lent is a planned disruption, albeit in a small way. So is a pilgrimage, where being taken out of your comfort zone, and the need to relate to others you journey with, provide a disruption to familiarity and thus a way of engaging with new perspectives. If people can understand what is involved in coming through a particular sort of difficulty, be it planned or not, and if struggle is embraced, it is easier to build resilience.

Struggle is an ongoing dynamic in the lives of the resilient. Although the abuse has ended, survivors of childhood abuse, for example, report struggling with depression, guilt, low self-worth, patterns of people pleasing and feeling overly responsible for others, difficulty in trusting, and challenges with establishing intimate relationships. The inner life of a typical survivor is a battleground where the forces of discouragement and the forces of determination constantly clash; and for many, determination wins out. Overcoming negative conditioning from childhood, such as a sense of shame or blame, is one aspect of the struggle. Voices from the past have been described as sirens which stir deepest longing, but are growth retardants if pursued. These sirens might be calling you to remember a harmonious upbringing, for example, and to deny that relationships within your family of origin were destructive or abusive. Meeting up with your family can then feel poisonous or defeating until you are able to recognize and mourn for what was lost. Sirens might be calling you back to believe what you were told as a child, that you were basically bad, or that whatever happens you mustn't cause a fuss.[7]

## SELF

The theme of self has within it many strands: change, self-esteem, autonomy, self-awareness, self-image, motivation, agency, autonomy or choice, the inner life, resourcing, and self-control and discipline. These aspects of the theme of self as it emerges in the literature on resilience are interwoven. To be resilient, a person must be able to change, and to adapt to new circumstances. Change requires motivation and the ability to sustain the demands that the change makes of self-esteem and self-image. Change begins with self-awareness, of the difficulty being faced and the emotional pain of its impact. Good enough self-esteem is vital in order to be motivated to come through and control, and empowerment enables resilience to be built. Self-control or discipline, as well as a rich inner life, helps a person to make choices and set a new direction. Factors related to the theme of self which I shall focus on from the wealth of material on the self are change and openness, self-esteem and control, and the resourced and disciplined self.

### Change and openness

Resilient people are those who are self-aware enough to know that change is necessary and are open to it. Robert Jay Lifton put forward a concept of the Protean self which emphasizes the need to change in order to be resilient, and he outlines what helps to bring it about. Using the motif of Proteus, the Greek sea god of many forms, he describes the Protean self as a self of many possibilities, which is able to tap human resiliency and flourish in the face of the dangers and confusions that can lead to the fragmentation of the self. The Protean or resilient self is an open self which involves vulnerability to painful feelings. As resilience builds such feelings will be felt and expressed authentically, intimate bonds with people will be formed and tough-mindedness and moral commitment engaged with. For though they may have experienced much pain and trauma during and after childhood, resilient people have been able to transmute that trauma into various expressions of insight, compassion and innovation. The resilient indeed continue to be motivated to change – to heal and grow personally as well as seeking change in their communities by social and political activity. They hold themselves accountable for their own recovery and are motivated for something more.

## Self-esteem and control

Self-aware enough to recognize that change is necessary in the face of adversity and be open to it, the resilient are those who have a good enough sense of self to be motivated to take up the struggle and the ability to do so. Self-esteem and control are key factors in building resilience. The innate or gut belief that survivors of abuse have that they were and are valuable and worth something is a strand that comes through the literature.

The significant resiliency themes include:

- the ability to find emotional support;
- self-regard or the ability to think well of oneself;
- spirituality;
- inner-directed locus of control.

Resilient survivors of childhood abuse report an unshakeable conviction that they deserve love, that good love exists and they can find it. This endurance of hope and the regulation of self-esteem are two hugely important resilience traits. Good enough self-esteem gives a person motivation to take up the struggle to survive, that is, to cope and to be constant in the face of destructive forces and then to reconstruct one's self-image and life.

The resilient come through and reject the version of self often described as *victimhood*, by continuing to revise their sense of self.

Constructing and deconstructing a view of themselves as victim is regarded by the resilient as a keystone of their recovery: once you were a victim with no control over your life, but now you are a *survivor* with solid control. To be healed you must first see that you were terribly hurt and fully recognize the extent of the damage. You need to get furious and outraged abut your maltreatment in order to place responsibility where it belongs and stop internalizing the rage and guilt that form the nearly inescapable legacy of abuse. You gradually learn (and trust) that you can become appropriately confrontational. Much of the adult growth of the resilient who were victims of childhood abuse, studies show, revolves around issues of self-esteem, of allowing themselves the same compassion that they extend to others. This sense of being a survivor rather than a victim, of being in control of one's life, is borne out by research into motivation in the form of self-determination theory. This has revealed that motivation and mental health are promoted when the psychological needs of competence, autonomy and relatedness are fulfilled. Without these, motivation and wellbeing decline. Motivation concerns energy, direction and persistence, and when choice, acknowledgement of feelings and opportunities for self-direction are present it increases. For those who have suffered childhood abuse, the struggle to become a survivor rather than a victim is hard won. Self-sufficiency and self-reliance, once virtues born of necessity, are later often overdetermined and outdated, so that now it is healthy interdependence that becomes the goal.

There have been numerous studies that have emphasized the importance of perceptions of the self and of agency and control in survivors of trauma, as we have seen in the experience of Viktor Frankl. Loss of control is a painful aspect of adversity and recovery involves regaining self-determination. For survivors of childhood abuse, recognizing personal power or internal locus of control might be expressed by the ability to take steps such as leaving home, setting limits, listening to their inner voice, making decisions and taking responsibility for themselves. Such steps have enabled the abused to stop and to overcome their traumatic experiences. In therapy, enabling clients to understand and trust the resiliency process empowers a client with an important sense of control in his or her life.

## The resourced and disciplined self

Openness to change, self-esteem and control are supported by a resourced self. A resilient self is one fuelled by a creative inner life and vision, as we have seen in the experience of Viktor Frankl where the motivation to survive took priority, but was easily lost if an inner life, or faith in the future, was lost. A vision of his personal future and the contemplation of love sustained Frankl. Other studies show that, for the resilient, overcoming is sustained by faith in surmounting and faith in relationships.

Resilience literature reveals the importance that religious faith can have in enabling people to overcome difficulty by giving them faith to hold on to life and find meaning and purpose, as well as by providing a supportive network of people. Prayer and meditation can be an integrating and creative process. Therapists in the studies often encourage prayer for those for whom it is an option, and faith in the form of a belief in personal destiny is seen by some as the most vital ingredient of resilience. A resourced self draws on positive perceptions of the self, and a vision of a different and better life which may be fuelled by religious faith or by books and the imagination and by activities that support resilience. These activities enable people to re-evaluate, consider and redirect their lives. They include a change of environment such as going on holiday, deferring judgement when faced with a problem in order to simmer or mull over the next step and thus broadening the quantity of possible solutions to a problem, and being alone. Solitude can facilitate changes of attitude and be as therapeutic as emotional support in some circumstances, such as in bereavement.

One way in which the self is resourced is through self-discipline. Though it is an unpopular concept in a materialist world propelled by consumerism and expectant of instant gratification, self-control or self-discipline is critical in resilience and can be learnt by practice. Self-control is defined as the self's ability to alter its states and responses. Since self-control is central to most forms of virtuous behaviour it can be regarded as the primary or master virtue. It seems to operate like a muscle which is weaker after exertion and replenishes with rest, slowly becoming stronger with repeated exercise and also strengthened by social support. For those in adversity, self-discipline during times of trauma can enable physical escape or psychological protection. After trauma self-discipline helps to deal with anger and hurt, setting boundaries in relationships and the rebuilding of life, as when survivors of childhood trauma make an ongoing, deliberate choice to manage their anger and hurt.

## RELATIONSHIPS

The kind of relationships that people have is hugely significant in the study of resilience. For many of the resilient, abusive relationships in earlier life have been the causes of adversity. Relationships, however, are a major factor in enabling people to build resilience, and as we have seen it is love and faith in relationships that often provide the vision to overcome.

Relationships during the period of difficulty are vital for overcoming. Resilient children are the ones who are adept at recruiting people as surrogates by their skill, appeal and determination, mostly from unofficial relationships outside the family. These frequently fleeting figures ignite the capacity of the children to love and provide sources of hope. They can give children a sense that they are deeply special and important. In adolescents, resiliency is encouraged by a wider network of relationships. The relationships that help the resilient as adolescents are those that provide an evaluative and reflective framework where they can begin to understand how and why their homes were different and explore their own disillusionments and pain, and where autonomy and competence are promoted. Other relationships are also of great importance to resilient children, such as relationships with peers in childhood, with siblings and friends and even animals. These relationships offer solace and mutuality and allow these children the opportunity to be helped themselves and to help others. Helping others also allows caregiving nourishment to be felt by the young helper, albeit vicariously.[8]

In reconstructing a new life, those people who are resilient see healthy relationships as vital. The quality of relationship that supports children in traumatic situations is that of Carl Rogers'

...ional positive regard'. Surrogates were those who encour-
...ged the resilient to let their talents unfold and conveyed not only
warmth and respect, but their own effectiveness as human beings
who also overcame hardship gracefully. One important quality
that surrogates had was avoiding placing the resilient in unten-
able loyalty conflicts.

Resilient adults seek relationships with people who avoid either
a self-sacrificial or self-referential imbalance in their ties, forming
relationships with overall reciprocity, respecting personal boundaries and avoiding inappropriate dependence. As adults the resilient are dedicated to creating depth of contact in all human relationships, recognizing the restorative power of human bonds and that
creating irreplaceable attachments is fundamentally humanizing.

The negotiating of right relationships is a struggle but the spiritual integrity of the resilient depends on limit setting. Part of the
process of rebuilding a sense of self involves receiving respect and
praise from others. It also involves minimizing contact with those
who diminish you. Setting limits, truthfulness, and resistance to
harm in relationships, for example with abusive families of origin,
enable personal growth and to neglect them is a growth retardant.
The resilient gradually learn to set limits and trust that they can
become appropriately confrontational, neither repeating family
patterns of the past nor colluding in them.

## FROM ADVERSITY TO ALTRUISM

In exploring the ways in which the lives of the resilient are shaped
by their struggle, their sense of self and their relationships, I
noticed that a process had emerged. Growth, that began in adversity and continued as resilience, was being expressed in altruism.
The direction of growth for the resilient includes moral connotations and carries with it assumptions about what it means to live
well and give well. Living well includes loving well, considering
one's life to be worthwhile and making a contribution. The resilient also give well and are involved in altruistic activity, such as
mentoring and working in the caring professions.

A reading of the literature points to some of the ways in which
transformation can come about, related to the struggle to grow

and heal, the sense of self and relationships with others. Resilient individuals journey from adversity to altruism, through a process which involves a new understanding of themselves. This enables them to develop empathy and then, by participation in altruistic activity, to direct their energies towards healing.

Therapy of various kinds is an important aspect of healing for many of the resilient, as is evidenced by the number of psychiatrists and therapists involved in writing on resilience as well as many of the resilient reporting how therapy has helped them. Therapy has enabled growth and healing in the resilient by the example of the person of the therapist, the nature of the relationship and the ability to gain a new perspective on themselves. Healing emerges partly from just sitting there with someone who can be seen in non-verbal ways as comfortable with him- or herself, who has a sense of self-worth, cares for others, and isn't self-focused. The one-to-one relationship of unconditional positive regard and trust can enable a survivor to rebuild trust in other human relationships by addressing the trauma of the past and seeking to heal and grow.

The process of healing involves a commitment to altruism which comes from a sense of self and an ability to empathize. Empathy is a quality of the resilient which involves decentring, a stepping back from one's own involvements sufficiently to enter into the mind of another. To decentre, a person needs previously to have been centred; a fragmented self is uncentred and struggling to keep itself together. The resilient give because they care, not out of martyred self-sacrifice, but because they have developed a healthy view of themselves.

The resilient involve themselves in altruistic activity because of their empathy and compassion and they report that healing for themselves is found through helping. Altruism has a transformative power, offering a better alternative to self-absorption or self-sacrifice for the resilient. Altruism is the foundation for ongoing health as well as providing an intense pleasure and a sense of spiritual satisfaction. Altruism, or morality, goes beyond the healing of an injured self. Morality is the last of Wolin and Wolin's seven characteristics of resiliency, the other six of which are: Insight, Independence, Relationships, Initiative, Humour and Creativity.[9] They describe morality as going beyond healing the self to improving the world.

Altruistic living has a regenerating power that enables healing. The resilient are those who have learnt to transform anger, avoiding the destructive polar extremes of depressive self-attack or sociopathic vengeance against others, and to transmute their trauma into various expressions of insight, compassion and innovation.

## FORGIVENESS AND HUMILITY

Important Christian virtues, particularly those of forgiveness and humility, are addressed by resilience literature – but from a different and challenging perspective. Healing emerges through altruism and through individuals' understanding themselves and their abusers, but not necessarily by forgiving them. The need to focus energy on healing the self means that forgiveness is not cited as being important in the process of healing. On the contrary, forgiveness can hold back healing because it concentrates energy on the perpetrator of abuse and derails healing, whereas understanding of the circumstances and the perpetrator can aid reframing and allow the survivor to move towards healing.

Humility, seen as deliberately cultivating a sense of unworthiness, is not a quality desirable for the resilient, who often struggle with a sense of unworthiness, shame and guilt. Resilient individuals are rather characterized by their ability to rebuild self-esteem after the knocks of adversity. Studies in humility as a virtue, however, have brought an understanding of the quality which resonates with the experience of the resilient. Humility is a rich, multifaceted construct. June Tangney describes it as involving:

- an accurate assessment of one's abilities and achievements;
- the ability to acknowledge one's mistakes, imperfections, gaps in knowledge and limitations;
- openness to new ideas, contradictory information and advice;
- a keeping of one's abilities and accomplishments in perspective;
- a relatively low self-focus, a 'forgetting of the self', recognizing that one is but one part of the larger universe;
- an appreciation of the value of things, as well as the many different ways that people and things can contribute to our world.[10]

The concept of humility is enriched rather than diminished by religious understandings, she argues, because the religious perspective describes one's place in the world in relation to God, so that one can be smart, but not all-knowing, and have personal power, but not omnipotence. There is a connection between humility and compassion which resonates with the observations already make about empathy. Humility, viewed positively, leads to compassion because of self-forgetfulness, rather than a self-focus that can come with false humility. Thus humility is not a devaluation of oneself but an increase in the valuation of others.

## RESILIENCE AS A CHALLENGE TO CHRISTIAN FAITH AND PASTORAL PRACTICE

There are particular criticisms of Christianity given in resilience literature which come from the experience of those who have suffered in childhood, though there is also the sense that Christian faith gave grounding in human decency, integrity and character. Criticisms include aspirations to infinite self-sacrifice and unreflective compliance, unfounded accusations and guilt-engendering admonitions, the tenet of original sin, and the perception of sex as sin. Though compassionate clergy quietly sheltered those suffering, many others felt betrayed by particular church officials who knew the gravity of their troubles and yet failed to challenge – or even condoned – their abusive home lives or preached general beliefs that amplified their parents' harshness. Several subjects in a study by Gina O'Connell Higgins said that organized religious teachings simply did not help enough with their unliveable home lives.[11] These criticisms need to be met with appropriate interpretations of the Christian understanding of concepts around obedience, self-denial, self-sacrifice, sin and guilt, and the body.

There are challenges to Christian theology and practice which arise around the themes of struggle, self and relationships. Struggle is central to growth and change and the building of resilience. Christian theology and practice should take account of pain and struggle, but not glory in them. Christian culture that proposes and expects that the better or more devout Christian should always be at peace, always feel full of trust in God and never be desperate needs to be challenged. An understanding of the place of obedience and trust needs to be addressed so that the vitality of struggle is not undermined and passivity encouraged.

The emphasis on self in resilience literature challenges a generalized doctrine of human nature and sin which might well promote a sense of unworthiness, punishment and shame that undermines the sense of self necessary for coping with adversity. This will include a nuanced view of the virtue of humility. Theological traditions that express a static view of the human person or emphasize tradition to the extent of resisting change will be challenged by the emphasis in resilience literature on the need to be open to change. Christian theology is challenged by resilience literature to give an account of human nature that does not emphasize sin to the extent of seeing little good in human nature and thus little capacity for strength and decision-making ability. Christian theology is challenged to emphasize the creativity and resourcefulness of human beings made in the image of God, rather than emphasizing sin and potentially glorifying suffering, passivity and victimhood.

With regard to pastoral practice, the self needs to be resourced and disciplined to build resilience. This challenges Christian pastors to present the Christian vision of the kingdom of God on earth and in heaven in such a way as to resource people and to promote self-discipline, recognizing that a spiritual practice such as giving something up for Lent is a planned disruption to life that promotes growth and prepares people to face adversity.

Much has been written on the need for appropriate relationships in churches, such as pastoral relationships and the boundaries important to observe, or the documents regarding the safeguarding of children and vulnerable adults. Resilience literature provides a challenge for Christians to nurture resilience by being available to be recruited by those in adversity as well as seeking to protect the vulnerable.

The need for people to withdraw from relationships that oppress them is clear in resilience literature. This has implications for theology and pastoral care relating to divorce and domestic violence, as well as what is taught about power, gender and family life. Great care needs to be taken with regard to teaching about forgiveness.

Pastoral relationships, in order to support resilience, need to be ones that can contain and support the process involved in personal change with its fluidity and emotional extremes. This will involve commitment to be alongside those in adversity with patience and without judgement. The importance of agency and choice challenges the pastor to listen rather than impose or prescribe, and to seek opportunities for those in adversity to exercise choice or agency in ways unrelated to their illness or difficult situation.

There is a theological challenge to Christian spirituality and pastoral care regarding trust. Resilience literature points to difficulties those who have experienced adversity have with moving from a necessary self-reliance to trust. Christian faith has trust in God at its heart. How to convey an understanding of God who relates to human beings in love and can be trusted, and also to enable such trust, must go far beyond a simple recommendation to trust God.

## Summary

In order to be strengthened in adversity, three themes from resilience literature are significant: struggle, self and relationships. The themes form the foundation for exploring how pastoral care can help people be strengthened in adversity. The literature identifies the need to embrace struggle and withstand the emotional pain that goes with it. To be resilient people will have a sense of themselves as having worth, control and an inner life resourced by a vision of a future that is better and different. Self-awareness and discipline go with the self-esteem necessary to face and come through adversity. Relationships with those who support and guide help, not least by fuelling the vision of a different way of life, because they have come through.

Resilience literature provides profound challenges to Christian theology and the emphases in pastoral care that can flow from theological concepts. Through the conversation partners that follow, these challenges will be explored and met.

# CHAPTER THREE

# The desert: landscape and metaphor for developing resilience

## THE DESERT AS A CONVERSATION PARTNER

In order to discover how best to help people be strengthened when they encounter adversity in their lives, we have looked at studies of resilience and heard how resilient people have come through difficulty. We have discovered that resilience is a process that involves a journey from adversity to altruism. We saw that the kinds of differences a church community and pastoral care can make are to do with attitudes to struggle, the self and relationships. This will impinge on preaching and teaching which will need to resource people with a vision of a life beyond their adversity, such as the kingdom of God and heaven. It will also involve promoting self-discipline and recognizing the importance even of fleeting relationships that convey to children and adults their worth, and give hope of a different way of living. We have been challenged by studies in resilience to be cautious about concepts like obedience and humility.

Having heard from studies in resilience, we now look to the Bible to discover how people have been strengthened in adversity. In the Bible, it is the portrayal of the desert experience that emerges for me as providing rich material to draw on, initially because of the way in which being in a desert resonates with the experience of adversity.

In this chapter, I shall look first at how the desert is presented in the Bible and at the narratives of Hagar and Moses. Here we find the desert as both a refuge and a place of adversity that enables them to face themselves and their situation and be strengthened by God. Their stories continue so that they become people who, having 'been there', live altruistically and take up pastoral responsibility. Having looked at the dynamics of strengthening in the stories of Hagar and Moses we will look at the desert itself. The physical landscape of the desert provides its own resilience process, as I was to find on an eight-day retreat in the Egyptian desert. Drawing on the biblical portrayal of the desert experience and the experience of the landscape, I will show how desert can be used as a metaphor for a three-stage process of being strengthened. This process resonates with what studies in resilience also point to. The desert metaphor, which we so often come across in the Bible, can help people to understand something of how their experience of adversity might be a journey on which they are strengthened.

## THE DESERT IN THE BIBLE

In the biblical tradition the desert stands as a physical place of adversity where God is encountered and where God provides both physically and spiritually. It is often adversity that causes someone to be in the desert, an adversity mirrored by trying to survive in the desert, or some sense of radical change to be faced that drives a person there. Thus the desert is not only a place of adversity, but a refuge where one can go to seek transformation.

The terms 'wilderness' and 'desert' are interchangeable when translated from the biblical languages into English although they are translations of several different words. The Hebrew words refer to different types of landscape, not all of which are uncultivated or uninhabited, but include pasture lands (1 Samuel 17.28). They can refer to large defined areas such as the Arabian and Sinai deserts (Genesis 14.6), as well as barren areas. 'Desert' refers to the desolation and ruin of waste places (Psalm 102.6), to dry land (Psalm 78.17), or to a vain or empty place (1 Samuel 12.21). In the New Testament the desert or wilderness is described as a deserted or lonely place (Mark 1.35, 6.31–32). Not only is there a varied geographical description of desert or wilderness, but there is a figurative use too, such as when the desert is described as a stormy and desolate sea in 'The oracle concerning the wilderness of the sea' (Isaiah 21.1). Difficult though the terrain may be, God's power extends to the wilderness (Psalm 107.35); and for the prophets, such as Elijah, it is a place of theophany (1 Kings 19.4). The theological development of wilderness is rich and no simple distinction can be made between its positive and negative connotations. In the wilderness wanderings from Exodus to Numbers God provides guidance in the form of a pillar of cloud and of fire (Exodus 13.21–22) as well as food and drink (Exodus 16.4). Hardships are seen positively as divine discipline (Deuteronomy 8.3–5). Many biblical narratives portray the desert as a refuge for individuals or whole communities to escape to in order to reassess their situation and set a new direction. For Hagar, Moses, the newly freed Israelite slaves and Elijah, physical danger and threat preceded their arrival in the desert, and the desert affords them protection and an experience of God who provides materially and spiritually.

In the New Testament, neither John the Baptist nor Jesus goes to the desert because of adversity, though that is what they encounter there and they emerge changed. John goes to the desert to live, undergoing the hardship of surviving and shaping his vision of a way of living pertinent to the age. His message was one of repentance or radical change, which he preached to the people, drawing on the image from Isaiah of a voice crying in the wilderness, so that his desert life drew on the desert spirituality of the prophets (Isaiah 40.3). Jesus is driven to the desert by the Holy Spirit after the experience of hearing God's voice affirming him at his baptism. After 40 days and 40 nights of fasting and temptation he emerges to begin his ministry. For Jesus, the desert was a place of physical and spiritual difficulty. Here wild animals lurked and Jesus was tempted by the devil and helped by angels. It was a place of adversity and strengthening which heralded change in his own life as well as in the lives of others (Mark 1.12–13). For both Jesus and John the desert was a place they entered alone, experiencing self-discovery through solitariness and suffering; and emerging from the desert they both turned to building a community of disciples.

The desert is a place of struggle that provides an encounter with the self and relating to God which leads to an inner strengthening and then re-engagement with others. This is the case in the narratives of Hagar and Moses, which also contribute to an understanding of the role of adversity in the development of altruism and pastoral responsibility.

## DESERT NARRATIVE: HAGAR

Hagar, a slave girl, is described as Egyptian in Genesis and so had probably been acquired by Abraham's household there. Her name, however, has a Semitic origin which may mean 'flight' and perhaps anticipates her later actions. Hagar was the handmaid of Sarah, Abraham's wife who, though her husband had been promised a son, remained infertile. Although the infertility of Sarah is the central issue in the narratives in Genesis they may equally well be read as a story centred on Hagar.

Genesis contains two narratives about Hagar (16.4–15 and 21.9–21). Each falls into two parts. In the first part of each scene Sarah, Abraham's wife and Hagar's mistress, directs her husband Abraham to a course of action in an attempt to secure her with a son and heir. These actions result in adversity for Hagar. The second part of each scene finds Hagar in the desert or wilderness and depicts an encounter with God. In the first scene, the desert or wilderness is a hospitable but a fleeting place, whereas in the second it is hostile and a place where she must remain. Hagar's story is steeped in adversity. The desert is a part of this reality and the place of self-assessment, change and strengthening.

In the first scene, Sarah gives Hagar to her husband, to secure her as a surrogate mother in accordance with the customs of the time. On becoming pregnant, Hagar, in a narrative full of images of sight, looks down on her mistress, and Sarah then oppresses and humiliates her. The words used of Sarah's treatment of Hagar are used later to describe the way in which the Egyptians treat the Israelite slaves. The pregnant Hagar flees to the wilderness, to Shur, not far from the Egyptian northeast boundary, to a place of refuge from adversity that is also a route on the way to her home. Here Hagar encounters a man, described as an angel of the Lord who is none other than God in human form. Such an appearance in Genesis nearly always comes to bring good news and salvation and tends to appear at moments of dire personal crisis, such as when Abraham is just about to sacrifice Isaac (Genesis 22.11). For Hagar this angel comes with a harsh order and a divine promise. He acknowledges her as a person by using her name, but by describing her as Sarah's maid reaffirms her social status. Hagar honestly admits to fleeing from her mistress and she is told not only to return but to submit, a word with the same root as humiliate and oppress, and the one used of Sarah's previous abuse of Hagar. She is promised a son. Ishmael means 'God hears'. God has heard Hagar, and shown he cares, but he does not liberate her from oppression.

Despite the mixed message of promise and suffering, Hagar's response to her encounter with God strengthens her to obey and return. She responds to God by being the only person in the biblical tradition to give a new name to God, El-roi, 'the one who sees me'. She also names the well in the wilderness, Beer-lahai-roi, 'the well of the living one who sees me', to mark the place where she has encountered God who sees her suffering and yet requires her to return to it with a promise of a future. It is in her moment of greatest distress that Hagar discovers God's concern for her and, strengthened in spirit, she returns to Abraham and bears a son.

In the second narrative involving Hagar, Ishmael is 'playing' with Isaac. This might be laughing with, indeed 'isaacing' with Isaac (for his name means laughing), or mocking him. Sarah, fearing that the eldest son Ishmael will take all or some of her son's privileges and inheritance, schemes to rid herself of him and his mother by driving them out. Abraham, reluctant to banish his son, but understanding it to be God's will, gets up early to say goodbye and provides mother and teenage son with bread and a skin of water.

Suffering divorce, banishment and the prospect of death, Hagar wanders in a wilderness that is not a place of refuge or exodus, but of exile: it does not border her homeland and, unlike Shur, Beersheba does not provide water. 'Wandering' implies that they are lost, and when Hagar sits down by herself the sense is of her isolation, uncertainty, lack or loss of direction, loneliness and parting. Desperate, and not able to bear to see her child die, she raises her voice and weeps, but she does not actually cry out to God. Unlike Moses, Ishmael does not see God in the bush under which he lies. Hagar is not heard by God but God does respond to Ishmael's cries, not by appearing as a physical presence but as a voice from heaven. Hagar hears the promise that her descendants will be a great nation and that she has a role to play. She who was under Sarah's hand (Genesis 16.6, 9) must now grasp Ishmael's hand. The earlier angel had predicted that Ishmael's hand would be against all, but that is not to include Hagar. Hagar then sees the well which symbolizes the provision of God for them. The renewed faith in God brought about by this encounter, which includes the promise that God's protecting hand will be over her son, leads to renewed purpose and action. Hagar shoulders the responsibility of parenthood, shown by her arranging a marriage for Ishmael. They make their home in the wilderness. Its territory provides work and Hagar's actions provide Ishmael with a future.

A resilience reading of the life of Hagar as depicted in Genesis shows the desert or wilderness to be both a place of refuge from adversity and a place of exile and adversity where a home must be made. The desert is the place where she finds direction and sets priorities for the future. In both cases it is a place of strengthening, through Hagar's acknowledging the grim circumstances of her life and encountering the divine who provides physically and spiritually. There is the struggle with adversity that causes her to flee to the desert, and the adversity of struggling to survive when she gets there.

Hagar has been depicted in different ways by the religious traditions that revere her. Once honoured for her obedience and suffering, she has come to be an inspiration for those in adversity who are seeking to cope by embracing the struggle by faith in a God who will strengthen them though not necessarily liberate.

In Christian theology the stories of Sarah and Hagar have been interpreted allegorically by St Paul with Sarah representing promise and freedom and Hagar law and slavery (Galatians 4.21–31). The theme of obedience is prevalent in interpretations of the narratives. Sarah is revered for her obedience: women who submit to their husbands in doing so become her daughters (1 Peter 3.1–6). Luther commends Hagar for returning home to obey Sarah, having been changed by her encounter with the divine messenger from her haughtiness and ingratitude. He exonerates Abraham for sacrificing conjugal and paternal love in order to obey and love God alone. Calvin too commends Hagar for her obedience to the divine messenger who corrects her faults of servile temper and indomitable ferocity, and describes her praying with words of self-reproach when she called upon God. Hagar has also been compared by Christian commentators to Mary, obediently accepting God's word and thereby bringing blessing to descendants too many to count.

Obedience is the quality for which Hagar has been revered in the Judeo-Christian tradition, her obedience to God in returning to her life of slavery and oppression. For the post-Christian feminist theologian Phyllis Trible, the narratives about Hagar are one of her studies in 'texts of terror', because Hagar does not receive liberation from God, but is ordered to return to oppression and so becomes the suffering servant, the precursor of Israel's plight under Pharaoh. For Trible, Hagar is a fleeting yet haunting figure in Scripture, her life depicting oppression in the three familiar forms of nationality, class and sex. She thus becomes a symbol of the oppressed, most especially of all sorts of rejected women who find their stories in hers. Though she is the first person whom an angel visits, the first to receive an annunciation and the only one to name God, she experiences exodus without liberation, revelation without salvation, wilderness without covenant, wandering without land, promise without fulfilment and unmerited exile without return.[1]

Hagar's life emphasizes an important aspect of resilience: that strengthening in adversity does not necessarily result in liberation from adversity. For other strands of Christian theology, along with the Hagar tradition in Islam, it is initiative, agency, fortitude and faith, rather than obedience, that are the qualities which bring strengthening. These are the qualities that cohere with the findings of resilience literature and they emerge from readings of the narrative from perspectives where adversity is experienced, due to a lack of power and social location.

For many generations African American Christians have drawn on the life of Hagar to identify models of faith, courage and hope as a promise that God participates in the human struggle for freedom. Hagar's predicament involved slavery, poverty, ethnicity, sexual and economic exploitation, surrogacy, domestic violence, homelessness, single parenting and radical encounters with God, and it has resonated with the experience of black American women.

Delores Williams argues that the biblical appropriation involving Hagar expands the community's knowledge of God's activity in the world. It shifts the dominance of faith in the Liberator God to an acknowledgement of God involved in the daily survival and quality-of-life struggle of black American women, since Hagar was not liberated but received new vision to see survival resources where she had seen none before.[2]

Hagar, of course, has an important place in Islam. That her story is known by a much wider range of people than Christians means that pastors in settings such as hospitals and prisons can refer to Hagar's example knowing that it will be recognized. Though the Qur'an does not mention her by name, in the Hadith Islam reveres Hagar as a woman of true faith, a messenger appointed by the one true God, and who is buried at the Ka'bah in Mecca. Hagar is depicted as walking between two mountains in the wilderness, with the angel Gabriel, or Jibreel, appearing to her on the seventh occasion. She emerges from the traditions as a 'woman of exceptional faith, love, fortitude, resolution, and strength of character', who 'does not see herself as a victim', but 'is a victor who, with the help of God and her own initiative, is able to transform a wilderness into the cradle of a new world dedicated to the fulfilment of God's purpose on earth'.[3] The Muslim theologian Hibba Abugideiri points to Hagar's life as providing moral lessons, real experiences and a model of leadership relevant to contemporary Muslim women. This they can have by drawing on the tool of Hagar's and their own empowerment, which is spiritual access to the divine. Hagar effected real change by *taqwa*, faith: not simply faith in God, but what the *taqwa* of Muslim women can inspire them to accomplish – a re-establishing of female agency. Hagar exemplifies the notion of active *taqwa*. God intervened to nourish Hagar because of her efforts to find help on her own, for activism and self-initiation are integral aspects of *taqwa*, not simply passive faith in God. Her struggle in the wilderness when left by Abraham to fend for herself was characterized by her constancy and God consciousness which, aided by her encounter with the archangel Gabriel, transformed initial panic and fear into relief and acceptance of the divine plan. Abraham's prayer for her safety was answered (Qur'an 14.37), but not without Hagar's suffering.

Hagar struggles as a divinely appointed messenger. Like all the messengers of Islam she endured many trials during her mission, but for her it resulted in her being the mother of the Arabs and having a huge role to play in the birth of this entire civilization.[4]

Hagar's strengthening takes the form of self-encounter and divine encounter. At the end of her tether, Hagar encounters herself, her situation and God. God hears her, names her, notices her suffering, provides for her and strengthens her to be able to obey the command to return to her adversity knowing that although there will still be humiliation, there is also promise. The encounter with God causes Hagar to recognize her own worth and, through the promise, be strengthened by a vision of a different kind of future, including a son who is free and whose line will continue. Returning to adversity requires the ability to withstand emotional pain and exercise self-discipline so that Hagar might provide a safe place to deliver and bring up her child. Living in the desert when Ishmael is grown also results in altruism or care for others, in the form of Hagar's caring for her son, providing him with a wife and being the mother of a nation.

Hagar's strengthening can be expressed in the 3Cs that resilience literature points to. It has physical aspects of being provided with water, meaning that the necessary *Coping* can be achieved. Promise and being named enable her to restrict the destructiveness of her situation and be *Constant*. She *Constructs* her new sense of self in order to go forward. Although Hagar returns to the adversity which will also be a place of safety for her and her unborn child, and in doing so obeys, she is not passive in this encounter, but an agent. The relationships that she needs are not easy, but necessary. The life of Hagar read through the lens of resilience literature reveals that it is not any virtue of obedience that is the source of her strength, nor her lack of liberation something that diminishes that strength. As contemporary African American Christian and Muslim women have found, it is through her courage to withstand difficulty and her encounter with God that she finds strength for herself to meet her circumstances.

## DESERT NARRATIVE: MOSES

The desert or wilderness features prominently in the life of Moses, most especially the 40 years of wandering in the wilderness. In the early chapters of Exodus, however, the wilderness features as the place to which Moses flees. The desert is the place where he makes a new life, encounters God and receives a call to give himself to the task of liberating others.

Adversity marked Moses' early life. He was rescued from infanticide by a plot devised by his parents and adopted by Pharaoh's daughter. Later, identifying with the Hebrew slaves, he killed an Egyptian slave driver, and having been discovered, needed to flee. Reading the life of Moses with the backdrop of resilience and the desert, at the stage of his life where he first encounters the desert, provides a biblical narrative of how a person can journey from adversity to altruism and gain maturity. This comes about by Moses' facing the adverse circumstances of life, out of which comes an inner strengthening in the form of an encounter with God and a call to serve and lead others. Moses' arrival in the desert coincides with supportive relationships, just as taking up his pastoral leadership does when it coincides with the emergence of his brother Aaron as a significant support. Just as the biblical narrative points to Hagar's experience as a precursor of that of the Israelite slaves, so too does Moses' experience. That Moses has 'been there' and come through gives him the credibility to take up pastoral leadership.

Moses journeys from adversity to altruism gaining maturity and wisdom along the way, which enables him to gain the trust of the people. His first attempt at helping his enslaved fellow Israelites lacks the moral undergirding required in order to be described as altruistic. His identity was bound up with the slavery of his people: this caused him to act, but he lacked the long-term vision, moral sense and altruism that characterize the resilient. When he tried to intervene in a dispute between two slaves his authority was rejected because of their fear that he would kill again (Exodus 2.14). To his chagrin, Moses discovered that his helping had made him an enemy and not an ally of his people, and so he had to flee to the desert. Moses flees and, having helped women who were being harassed by shepherds to water their flocks at the well, he receives the hospitality of the priest of Midian. The adversity of rejection and flight developed Moses' sense of empathy and justice. In this story three types of injustice are experienced in three incidents in quick succession: the slave is beaten to death by the Egyptian master, the neighbour is wronged by his Hebrew kinsman, and the male nomads deprive the women of their ability to get water. Moses' sense of justice develops to transcend boundaries of nationality, gender and kinship.

The journey from adversity to altruism is enabled by Moses' ability to struggle, relate to others and develop his sense of self. The adversity that led him to the desert shaped his moral sense and his experience of the desert enabled him to prepare to take up pastoral leadership. This was because he had shared in suffering at the hands of the Egyptians, had managed to survive in the adversity of the desert, and returned both to witness the slavery of his people and later to the desert, strengthened. The early passages of Exodus have an overarching theme of the preparation of the deliverer for his task, which involved his identifying with his people under oppression and finding a home in an alien land. Moses becomes one of them by virtue of his own experience.

Relationships enabled Moses to survive the adversity of the desert and to grow into someone who could be strengthened by adversity in an altruistic direction. Moses was shown considerable hospitality by strangers, as a result of his protection of the women he met at the well. He became a shepherd, married Jethro's daughter Zipporah and became a father. The name of his son, Gershom, indicates that Moses still remembers that he is a 'sojourner in a foreign land', belonging to another people in another land, but he had found a home away from home.

The desert enabled Moses to find a sense of self and reassess his life. The flight to a desolate desert, far from the marks and patterns of activity that had identified him in Egypt, was what he needed to reassess his identity and connections. The result of his reassessment, alone in the wilderness, was an encounter with God who directed him to a life of altruism and pastoral oversight. Moses noticed a common desert bush on fire and decided to go and look more closely. His encounter with God came in the midst of his everyday activity as a shepherd when he was presumably conscious of nothing more than his flock. He had driven his sheep well into the wilderness, beyond the customary routes of Midianite territory, and found himself on a mountain in the wilderness named Horeb, 'Wasteland', which became the place of revelation.

The encounter with himself and his situation in the desert, the support of others and time alone led Moses to an encounter with God (Exodus 3.1–12). The call was one he obeyed, but the encounter was not one where Moses was passive. God's presence was hospitable, respecting of autonomy and reassuring. Moses finds himself in a presence that invites him to be at home and at the same time claims his profound respect. Having experienced being an alien in a foreign land he finds himself a guest of God. Though Moses is afraid to look at God and hides his face, he is anything but deferential. Disagreement, argument and even challenge play an important role in the encounter. God does not demand a self-effacing Moses. God reveals himself not simply at the divine initiative, but in interaction with a questioning human party. Simple deference or passivity in the presence of God would close down the possibilities. Moses displays genuine modesty, but coupled with fear of the unknown and a tendency to make excuses, blame others, and ask questions not worthy of a prophet. Each of these is handled by God with the utmost seriousness, the objection examined and met with a divine promise (Exodus 3.13—4.31). God places the divine word and will into the hands of another for him to do with it what he will. That is for God a risky venture, fraught with negative possibilities. Moses is to return to Egypt where his compatriots are slaves and lead them to liberation.

The narrative of these first four chapters of the book of Exodus reveals Moses growing towards altruism through developing empathy and a sense of justice, from his experiences of adversity. The struggle with the memories of what he had done and the life he had lost was made productive by time alone in the desert as well as support by others, and this led to a reassessment of his life and an encounter with God.

In the experience of Hagar and the early experience of Moses in the desert we see that strengthening in adversity comes from an experience of desert which enables both to face their circumstances and themselves and encounter God, not passively but in a way that brings out their personhood and results in an altruistic task. This is not a path to personal liberation, but a return to adversity and a call to work for the good of others by hope in a future promised by a God in whom they trust.

## THE DESERT AS A LANDSCAPE

The Bible bears witness to many people who have been strengthened by God in the desert. Of course, much of the biblical narrative is set in the desert anyway. Desert, however, is more than just the geographical location. The landscape shapes the human person by forcing attentiveness to the external conditions and inner psychological and spiritual state in order to survive. This struggle to survive enables a person to set priorities, focus energy and in doing so be strengthened.

It is commonly held that deserts are areas of boundless plain, a monotonous and uniform landscape with constantly blowing sand. They are hot, with few life forms, and to be avoided. But although there are such regions, for the most part deserts do not fit such a description. Three kinds of surface characterize deserts: stony, sandy, and the adobe surface of rock particles, finer than sand and more common. Even in the Sahara desert it is estimated that sand does not cover as much as a third of the area. Rather than monotony, nearly all deserts contain striking contrasts of relief which include mountains and the gentle slopes that characterize the landscape. Heat is usual in the middle of the day, but it is cold at night. Desert is landscape that does receive rain – albeit less than ten inches a year – so that except in extreme instances there is varied and numerous animal and plant life. Rainfall of between 10 and 20 inches indicates a grass or steppe region, semi-arid, which in the dry season has a desert-like appearance, but in the rainy season has luxuriant vegetation.

The beauty of the desert consists of the intensity of the colours, the stars and moonshine of the nights, the silence and the purity of the atmospheric conditions, including the absence of odour either good or bad. Those human beings able to get in touch with their human and physical environment see a vastness and freedom that is sublime and awe-inspiring.

Living in the desert is difficult and requires daily life and travel to be carried out in ways that have been constant for centuries because they are the only ways of surviving. The desert exerts a strong and abiding influence on the habits and customs of peoples and the spirit and life of nations. The way of life of the Bedouin, who have been predominantly nomadic, is very well adjusted to the environment. Though pasture is uncertain, where there is enough rain, farming is possible. There is a severity in living nomadically where famine is common and where wealth consists only in owning flocks of sheep and goats. This and the necessary simplicity of life enable there to be a greater equality and uniformity between people.

There are those who flee to the desert, those who find themselves there unexpectedly and those who seek it. In each case the desert is experienced to be a great teacher. The model for desert Christians, St Antony, explicitly cited the desert as teacher when he was asked how he could live so far away from books: 'My book is the nature of created things: whenever I want to read the word of God it is always there for me,' he said, for it was the landscape of the desert that formed and defined his spirituality and being.[5]

There are classic writings on the experience of the desert landscape and the way in which it shapes human perspective, psychologically and spiritually. One is *Wind, Sand and Stars* by Antoine de Saint-Exupéry who landed in the Libyan desert in 1935. He describes what it took to survive in the desert: being meticulously observant, stubbornly indifferent to the panic and despair, and eventually being rescued by Bedouin, factors which express the significance of struggle, self and relationships for surviving. A spiritual classic is Carlo Carretto's *Letters from the Desert* where a life in the solitude and sparseness of the desert forms a spirituality of love and contemplation. Belden Lane, who has integrated his experience of the solace of fierce landscapes with his experience of his mother's dying, emphasizes the importance of the experience of harsh terrain especially at times of adversity and healing.

The study of spiritual traditions in relation to their particular geographies, spiritual or psycho-geography, is quite a recent phenomenon. Peter Brown describes monasticism in Syria and Egypt in the fourth and fifth centuries as assuming different forms because of variations in the desert terrain they occupied. In Egypt there was 'true desert', with a rainfall of only 1.1 inches a year. Sheer survival in such a hostile environment required structure, conformity and adherence to routine. By contrast, in the rugged, mountainous terrain of Syria, which was milder and less demanding than the Egyptian desert, the ascetic life would be characterized by greater individuality, freedom and the embrace of wildness, since less energy had to be absorbed in the onerous task of staying alive.[6] Other writers have explored the way in which the harsh terrain of desert shapes the spirituality of communities, especially with its effect upon healing. One of these is Kathleen Norris, who describes the spiritual geography of Dakota, reading spirituality and small-town culture from a desert landscape.

## A DESERT FEAST

My own experience of the desert landscape came when I went on an eight-day retreat to the Sinai Peninsula with the Makhad Trust in 2010. We were hosted by the Bedouin and slept without shelter, and the retreat included three days and nights when I was solitary and fasting. The retreat was not of any particular faith tradition and was entitled 'Desert Feast' to emphasize the sense of the fullness and provision of the desert. As I had expected, I found that the landscape of the desert itself taught me. It was in the need to attend to silence, to an indifferent landscape and to the changing physical conditions in order to survive that I learned something of the inner strengthening the desert is famous for enabling.

Being silenced is an experience common to those who have had traumatic experiences and were forced to keep quiet as well as perhaps being unable to find either language or opportunity to talk of their experience. Coming through the experience involves naming, acknowledging that one was silenced and now can talk and so experience healing in being listened to attentively, in being able to be a subject rather than an object. The desert is a noisy place where the wind fills the senses and where the sound of a voice crying out would be lost in the howling, silenced. It is also a place of stillness and silence where there is a desire to shout and make an impact on the terrain. Within, the retreatant is noisy with thoughts and feelings, but over some time begins to settle, by attending to the self in observation and care and attending to the landscape. Such awareness enables the person to move towards a place of inner silence and fullness. Silence is a spiritual discipline, but to be silenced is a destructive experience. Experiencing the landscape of the desert provides a process by which one can move from being silenced to a place of inner silence.

The desert experience can also be characterized by the movement between indifference and support. The landscape is stark and unforgiving; survival is a struggle with the extremes of the heat during the day and the cold at night. There appears to be no water or living things. The desert gives nothing and so the retreatant has to be resourceful in order to survive in a landscape indifferent to your plight. The same is true for the inner self since the desert is not only indifferent to your physical survival, but indifferent to your feelings or mental state. There is no one in the desert to praise or comfort you, no one for you to blame. And so one has to look within and face the demons, as we and the desert Christians might call them, who tell us we are worthless or justified, and then deal with the rage or sadness that may emerge when alone. And yet the land is supportive and such a realization is humbling. Indifference can be restorative, especially when there is no one to oppress or abuse, when you are left alone and liberated from any physical or verbal abuse inflicted by another. But the landscape is more than supportive because it does not deliberately harm you. The rock of the desert wilderness is rounded, feminine in shape. It provides shelter from the wind and cold, shade from the sun, a place to sit down. It is a refuge that invites the metaphor of God as a rock (Psalm 18.2, 42.9). Containment is an aspect of the support here. The desert, borderless and empty, contains the wildness, and it can hold the person in the process of expressing deep-seated violence and passion, so that it can be healed, tamed and directed.

The desert is a place of change as well as of stability. Aspects of the landscape constantly change – night and day, sun and moon, breeze and wind. These are both predictable and unpredictable, as is the fear that comes with night when it is impossible to imagine light, warmth or the relaxation that comes with the sun on the body. To survive psychologically and not be overwhelmed with fear one has to hold on to the belief that it will be warm or cool again. The changefulness is a constant and a person can learn to endure when it is uncomfortable, trusting that the natural process of the landscape will change again and bring relief, even comfort. It is also true to say that the desert does not change. The rocks stay, wise and ancient, moulded by the weather, but only over very long periods of time. Such change and the stability of the landscape cause one to consider what changes and what is stable, what is important, in human life generally and in one's own personal life.

A desert retreat, as in my case, will often be accompanied by solitary time and by fasting, because the vastness of the terrain and scarcity of food are part of the physical features. These contribute to attentiveness to oneself and one's surroundings. Physical factors are as important as the psychological in both the difficulties and the benefits. Being alone is neither a punishment nor an endurance test, but provides the opportunity for reflection. Solitary confinement is a torture, not because you are solitary, but because of the accompanying threats, uncertainty and lack of sleep, and most especially because of the sensory deprivation.[7] In the desert there is no sensory deprivation: indeed the senses are filled because the landscape is vast and beautiful. Fasting requires self-discipline, provides mental alertness and gives rest to the body, as sleep does, so that the energy normally used for digesting food can be used to cleanse the body of accumulated toxins and contribute to healing. Such detoxification of the body, of course, is quite commonly used in contemporary society by those who want to improve their health.

The landscape of the desert, and the kind of life that is possible there, provides its own resilience process. From being silenced, experiencing indifference and the unpredictability and fear that comes with change, the landscape itself teaches that one can come to a place of silence, support and stability. The landscape does not change, but the human being does as he or she determines the priorities needed for physical and psychological survival and wellbeing. The learning is a struggle that emerges from within, shaped by physical factors.

## THE DESERT AS A METAPHOR

The desert is a physical place where much of the biblical narrative is played out and a landscape which enables human beings to move beyond adversity to inner strengthening, but most human beings will not spend time in desert terrain. Their experiences of adversity, however, are analogous to finding oneself in the desert. Desert or wilderness functions as a rich metaphor. Metaphors are not just a characteristic of language, but are pervasive in everyday life and shape thought and action. Metaphors are rooted in experience and using them means we can pick out parts of our experience and treat them as distinct entities. This enables us to refer to them, categorize them and, in doing so, reason about them so that they enable us to partially structure one experience in terms of another in order to make our experience coherent. This is of course very important when experiencing adversity – the metaphor of the desert can help people to recognize their experience and see the path to a journey that can be strengthening. To use metaphor in speaking of faith can bring fresh insight which can be life-shaping, and is a crucial skill in creating rapport and in communicating the nature of unshared experience. Story and myth, image and symbol are all important so that implicit theology can become explicit. This means it can be critiqued and changed, so that, for example, a person might be given permission to struggle by the desert metaphor and in doing so find the motivation to survive.

## THE THREE MOVEMENTS OF THE RESILIENCE PROCESS IN THE DESERT METAPHOR

The metaphor of desert structures the experience of adversity into three movements of a resilience process. This is valuable to the pastor in enabling people to see the experience of adversity as a staged journey, and one through which they can be strengthened.

The three movements are:

- embracing the desert by acknowledging one's situation and the need to change;

- encountering the self and being strengthened;
- developing altruism and pastoral responsibility.

The first movement of embracing the desert is reflected in the landscape and the human response to it. The desert landscape is different from any other and to survive there you have to live differently. When we face a new and difficult experience in life, where we are alone in a place where demons lurk, the only creative choice is to embrace the struggle and make changes. When adversity strikes – for example, terminal illness or bereavement – we experience crossing into new terrain, a different space where new ways of living will be essential for survival.

The desert stands for any place of abandonment and aloneness. It is used metaphorically and psychologically for any place of solitude, simplicity and emptiness. Anyone who has experienced some aspect of deserted-ness, loneliness, brokenness, breakdown or break-up – whether emotionally, physically or socially – will be able to make the necessary connections to the desert. 'Desert' in English gives this sense of a deserted place, but the desert is not a neutral space. The experience of desert involves the experience of abandonment. It is a place of demons and where God seems absent. Faced with a new terrain, alone and with inner and outer difficulties to cope with, the choice that leads to survival is that of embracing the desert. To go through the desert experience involuntarily can be both overwhelming and crushing. To embrace it can prove both constructive and liberating.

*Embracing the desert* is acknowledging the need to survive brought about by the physical and psychological vulnerability of being alone in a barren landscape, be it real or metaphorical. There is nowhere to hide nor any room for lying or deceit in the desert of adversity if one is to survive, and the self is reflected by the desert landscape so that one has to face up to it. Remaining open to the threat that such vulnerability poses is vital, for certain truths can be learned, it seems, only as one is sufficiently emptied, frightened, or confused. This takes one to the second movement of the resilience process of the metaphor.

*Encountering the self and God* so as to be strengthened comes from recognizing that one's vulnerable self can be an experience of integration and growing in wholeness. From a place of vulnerability, people can be renewed and transformed. Many people seek an experience of adversity through desert spirituality. For those who choose the desert in order to grow in holiness the aim is often expressed by writers on spirituality as seeking to be stripped of self, to be purged by its relentless deprivation of everything once considered important, and to experience a purging that demands a deep sense of relinquishment. These writers recognize the desert as a metaphor of the place where you come through transformed, finding strength having encountered God. This aspect of the desert experience does not lend itself to description in the same way that the experience of adversity does, so it is as a metaphor that the desert has had a significant and continuous role in the history of Christian mysticism, with Western mystics using the metaphor of the desert to describe the impossible, that is, God and their encounter with God.

The third movement of the desert metaphor is that of *altruistic living and pastoral responsibility*. It is hinted at in the studies in resilience and present in the biblical desert narratives. We will also find it described in the texts of the desert Christians of the fourth and fifth centuries, particularly in the relationship between elder and disciple, and its dynamics are explored in the pastoral care of the wounded healer.

A key task of the pastor is to help people be strengthened in the adversities of their lives. This will mean enabling people to embrace the desert by recognizing the situation they find themselves in. It will mean helping them to look inwards, so that they can encounter themselves and God, and so reach for the motivation and energy to come through. It will also involve helping them to heal and live beyond themselves and what has happened into a new chapter of their lives. The pastor needs to be someone who has been on this journey personally and so can show the way.

## Summary

That the resilience process involves a journey from adversity to altruism through attention to struggle, self and relationships is affirmed by the biblical tradition. In attending to the question of how pastoral care can strengthen people in adversity, the Hagar narrative draws attention to the reality of the need for inner strengthening in chronic situations of adversity. The Moses narrative recognizes the importance of having 'been there' and of having this experience recognized by those who would accept pastoral ministry. Both narratives show clearly the experience of God revealed – for Hagar in extreme adversity and for Moses in a time of quiet. Personal affirmation and direction are part of the encounter, but in a way which respects autonomy, does not require passive obedience, and opens up a vision of a future that includes responsibility for the welfare of others. Biblical scholarship and commentary itself has begun to include the experiences of those traditionally not given a voice and the emphasis has shifted from obedience to autonomy. This shift indicates that Christian theology has already begun to respond to the criticisms from resilience literature of the impact of religious belief on the ability of people to be strengthened in adversity.

Through the experience of the desert as a landscape and a metaphor, in the past and today, the three aspects of the resilience process are revealed. Metaphors enable us to structure our experiences so that we can make sense of them. The metaphor of the desert provides a structure for the experience of adversity, of encounter with oneself and with God, and of strengthening in the direction of altruism.

As we have seen, the metaphor's most vivid and common use is that of describing adversity, particularly the way in which adversity marks a distinctive boundary to be crossed, different from what has gone before. The experience of strengthening in the desert is a natural extension of the metaphor, and though it is difficult to describe the attempt to do so is a recurring preoccupation of Christian spirituality. The third movement of the metaphor, altruism and pastoral responsibility as a means of healing and growth, remains to be explored.

# CHAPTER FOUR

# Desert Christians embrace adversity for growth

## INTRODUCTION

In the Bible, through the stories of Hagar and Moses, we have seen that the desert experience, both literally and metaphorically, enables us to make sense of the process of coming through adversity well. This builds on what we heard about the ways in which resilient children and adults find strength. Coming through adversity well and building resilience involves struggle, a good sense of self, which is both disciplined and resourced, and relationships with other people. I have proposed three stages of the desert metaphor which describe the process of growing in resilience and do so with attention given to struggle, self and relationships. The stages are:

* embracing the desert;
* encountering God and the self;
* altruistic living and pastoral responsibility.

Among the relationships with other people, the role of the pastor can be of enormous significance. That the pastor has 'been there', has experienced adversity and been strengthened by it, and has found that pastoral ministry brings healing, both for others and for the self, are all indications of resilience.

## A CONVERSATION WITH THE DESERT CHRISTIANS

Having looked at the experience of the desert as one that enables people to be strengthened in adversity, we now turn to the experience of the desert Christians of the fourth and fifth centuries. We shall discover how their way of life enabled them to turn adversity into compassion. The life and teaching of the desert monks and nuns bear witness to the processes we know the resilient go through and which bring strengthening. They do so in a Christian framework, albeit from long ago, and attest to the difficult and sustained struggles that are required to grow and develop in a moral and compassionate way, then and today.

It may be hard to imagine how the lives of monks and nuns living in the desert so many hundreds of years ago can have anything to say to us about how to come through adversity ourselves or help other people to do so. After all, didn't the desert Christians choose to go and live in the desert? We do not choose our adversities – they are unexpected and unwelcome and the solution is not to pack up and travel to desert territory. We have already learnt, of course, that the first step in coming through difficulty well is to choose and even to embrace the experience. We have also seen how the metaphor of desert resonates with the experience of adversity, of entering new terrain, of the need to survive, and of being alone in the experience.

The *Alphabetical Sayings* of the desert Christians that we shall look at in this chapter address the difficulties of embracing the desert. The practices and pithy teachings helped disciples to begin a new life in the desert that enabled them to encounter themselves and God within – stages one and two of the desert metaphor. Pastors, the desert tradition shows us, require specific qualities, beyond having 'been there' and come through well, and they encounter particular pitfalls. In turning to John Cassian we will discover resources which can help sustain the third stage of the desert metaphor, that of altruism and pastoral responsibility. John Cassian (360–435) developed and interpreted the ways of the Egyptian desert that he had experienced on his travels in his works, the *Institutes* and *Conferences*, in order to convey the wisdom of the desert to monks in Gaul where he had been charged with forming new monastic communities. His writings provide a model of resilient growth and living emerging from life in the desert, but he applied it to his own context and made the Christian vision explicit. Like us, he uses the desert as a metaphor for the way in which the monastic life enables growth and applies it to his context.

## DESERT CHRISTIANS IN EARLY CHRISTIANITY

In the fourth century so many people fled to the Egyptian desert and later to the desert south of Palestine that Bishop Athanasius of Alexandria could claim by 357 in *The Life of Antony* that 'the desert had been made into a city'. It was, in fact, the widespread success of Athanasius' work in particular, because it drew on the powerful metaphor of desert, that encouraged the movement to the desert. By the year 400 nearly five thousand monks were said to be settled in the Nitrian desert and many thousands were scattered up and down the length of the Nile and even in the bleak, waterless mountains of the Red Sea. By the mid-fourth century Egyptian Christianity had earned international fame. The writings and example of the desert Christians influenced monastic life for centuries, both in the Greek East and in the Latin West, and they remain popular in contemporary spirituality.

These Christians went to live in the desert prepared to embrace the adversity of the way of life. It used to be generally accepted that flight to the desert became a kind of substitute for martyrdom since being prepared to die as a martyr for Christ had become outdated. These desert Christians were thus called 'white martyrs' rather than the 'red martyrs' who had had their blood shed. As the Emperor and the Roman Empire had become Christian it was no longer a risk to be a Christian. Christianity became a respectable way of life and, with new relationships being forged with the authorities, complacency was in danger of setting in. Social and political conformity became the norm for Christians who began to feel at home in the world. Since life in the world had become comfortable for Christians, the desert became the place where struggle could take place. The desert provided shelter from the distractions of daily life and a place of stability and tranquillity so that demons could be confronted with a fixed mind and clarity of purpose. People went to the desert for many reasons, however; we are now aware that it was to flee from adversity as well as to embrace it. There is evidence that many fled to the desert in order to avoid persecution, making the desert a refuge from, as well as a place of, adversity. The ascetic life was also lived out in many places other than the desert itself. So going to the desert was not always a voluntary decision and the desert experience was not always in the landscape of the desert.

Some who actually went to the desert became anchorites or hermits. Both men and women left human society and sought the wisdom of an amma or abba in Lower Egypt, after the model of St Antony the Great. Others joined the cenobitic or communal type of monasticism of Upper Egypt which consisted of communities who prayed and worked together. None of these ascetics lived in isolation, even if some spent long periods of time alone, years even. Kinship, property, the deployment of labour and exchange of goods, along with links with the Church, provided emotional connections as well as economic dependence.

There were also urban monks or *apotaktikoi* (those who renounce) who functioned in a wide variety of circumstances and played an active role in villages and towns. Urban monks retained ties with churches and some had important roles in towns. The sources reveal their presence within towns and villages and indeed *The Life of Antony* shows him in the full range of ascetic roles: close to his native village, living among tombs, in a fortress, and then in the desert. The anchoretic and cenobitic monks, as well as the *apotaktikoi*, were all engaged in economic activity such as hiring themselves out at harvest, and weaving baskets and ropes. There were organized ascetic communities for women, some of which involved women leaving their families and some where the family was transformed to become an ascetic household that accepted non-related members.

Thus the popular understanding that Egyptian monasticism consisted of Antony the Great going into the desert to lead the life of a hermit where thousands flocked to him, living as hermits and in communities, is a myth, but a very powerful one. Christians renounced family, sex, property or business within the home, the village and the city, but it was only when ascetic practice began to take place expressly in the desert that the literature emerged and established the desert hermit as the literary icon of early Egyptian monasticism.

In the past and in the present people are drawn to the idea of the desert, though not necessarily to the place. In particular, it seems to be the way in which the desert represents different terrain and presents a boundary that must be crossed that resonates with the human experience of radical change. Desert Christians then, like contemporary Christians who find themselves in a difficult and uninviting place, do not always live in the desert. What the many Christians who took up the desert life, whether in the desert itself or in towns or at home, were doing was committing themselves to a way of life that involved making life more difficult for themselves in some way. They pursued adversity, renouncing aspects of their lives in order to grow in the practice of their faith. For many this did involve living in the landscape of the desert. For others the desert was a metaphor for a way of life that brought strengthening by embracing adversity.

We may well find ourselves very cautious about turning to the lives of the desert Christians. After all, how can these people who fled to the desert and renounced their former lives be any kind of example of coping with difficulties? Just as we do not expect to live in the desert, we do not think of faith as involving pursuing adversity or renouncing. However, we do find ourselves in the situation of having to renounce, though we may not use that word. We find ourselves needing to renounce, or acknowledge and then come to terms with, the loss of mobility or health or a relationship. We may find ourselves needing to exercise discipline over our diet in order to avoid illness and disease. In doing this we are pursuing a difficult, even an ascetic path, in order to benefit from a longer and healthier life. In turning to the desert Christians, we shall find a pattern not unlike the process of rebuilding resilience. We will also have to make some important readjustments to some common assumptions about the desert tradition of this period. The struggle with the adversity of asceticism and self-discipline, for example, is not a self-denial that crushes the human spirit but aims to provide for growth and healing. The self, we find, is not to be passively obedient and humble and thus vulnerable to abuse; rather, there is an emphasis on guarding and resourcing an inner life. Flight from relationships that are destructive is commended, but not a shunning of all relationships. Indeed, the relationship with the elder is vital for a strengthening in adversity to enable trust, rather than a destructive self-reliance. Read with the insights of resilience literature in mind we find that as the desert Christians embrace the desert they reveal a way of life where adversity can be strengthening.

## THE *ALPHABETICAL SAYINGS*

The lives and teaching of the desert Christians can help us to embrace the desert of adversity when it strikes. They show us a process or pattern and because it is an extreme one it is easy to see what matters. It is the *Sayings* collection that presents a Christian understanding and practice of facing adversity and growing through it.

The different collections of anecdotes about early Christian ascetics called *Alphabetical Sayings*, *Apophthegmata Patrum*, or *Sayings of the Fathers* come from within the desert and so give a sense of the practices of desert Christianity. The *Sayings* were collected from monastic leaders active from the 330s to the 460s though the texts probably come from the late fifth or early sixth century. Monks turned to them as well as to *The Life of Antony* for the stories and teaching to help make sense of their experiences of temptation, anxiety and sadness. The *Sayings* are records of practical advice given by desert elders, the abbas – the 127 male elders who contribute to the collection – and the three ammas, the female elders. There are 1,202 sayings in all coming out of a long life of experience in monastic and ascetic discipline in the desert.

The *Sayings* represent a type of ascetic formation built around an anchorite guide–disciple relationship exemplified by the use of the formula 'Give me a word'. That is what a disciple or pilgrim would ask of a desert elder. The 'word' given was timely and appropriate for the one who asked it, not a universal statement, but sayings were remembered and written down because others could also learn from them. The *Sayings* are thus not always consist-

ent with one another and they always need to be read with.
context in which they were given – the life-giving relationsh.
between an elder and a disciple. The relationship between disciple
and elder was vital for spiritual development, just as healthy relationships are vital for people experiencing adversity. The desert
was considered to produce healers rather than teachers or think-
ers. Just as in a good pastoral relationship, it is not teaching or
advice that is at the heart of what helps someone, but the listening
and responding that enables healing. That is why each Saying is
for the person to whom it is given, in the context of that particular
situation. It might be pertinent to another person, but it may not,
or not all the time.

## THE *SAYINGS* AND RESILIENCE

When you read the *Sayings* through the resilience themes of
struggle, self and relationships you find that the practical advice
and implicit theology support the emphases presented by resilience literature as vital to strengthening. These sayings provide
an example of Christians living out the first movement in the metaphor of embracing the desert. It was a long time ago, but their
advice to flee, sit, guard the inner life and practise asceticism can
speak to us today. This advice resonates with what we have heard
helps people face the difficult circumstances that life has thrown
up, but it isn't advice that we hear a lot about in church. There, I
suspect all too often, we pick up that God wants us to work slav-
ishly for others and not count the cost, rather than to flee from
those who diminish us or to guard our energy. Experiencing difficulty forces us to reconsider our lives. The desert Christians show
us how we can follow Christ while we meet the challenges facing
us. That will involve rethinking how we approach the themes of
struggle, self and relationships in one-to-one pastoral relationships as well as in teaching and preaching.

## STRUGGLING TO GROW

The desert Christians certainly address struggle as a theme. I shall look here at what the *Sayings* say about how we grow and I shall also touch on the subject of demons, who are encountered quite a lot in desert literature. The self-discipline of asceticism is a struggle in itself, of course, but I shall leave that until we get to the section on self.

The theme of growth through conflict enjoyed great prominence in the early monastic world, with the purpose of the monastic life being seen as providing a stable place geographically and psychologically where important battles could be fought. Struggle was the motif that the early Christians aspired to, following St Paul, with the image of the athlete engaged in competitive struggle to gain self-mastery in order to fight the enemies of Christ.

Struggle was sought because it was considered to be a spur to growth, and necessary for salvation. In the *Sayings* it was often described in the language of temptation: Amma Theodora encouraged disciples to seek adversity by saying:

> Let us strive to enter by the narrow gate. Just as the trees, if they have not stood before the winter storms cannot bear fruit, so it is with us; this present age is a storm and it is only through many trials and temptations that we can obtain an inheritance in the Kingdom of Heaven. (Theodora 2)

St Antony said: 'Whoever has not experienced temptation cannot enter into the Kingdom of Heaven.' He even added, 'Without temptation no one can be saved' (Antony 5).[1]

### Struggling with our demons

Demons appear in many of the *Sayings*. The battle for the monks and nuns was with demons and struggle involved both the body – with the monk or nun following the self-discipline of asceticism – and the mind. Demons and angels, invisible seducers or helpers, were a pervasive presence in the world of the desert Christians. The demon was a fearsome enemy that could appear as a wild animal or even an angel. Looked at psychoanalytically, of course, they can be understood as products of repression, projection and persistent anxieties. We talk about our demons today when we want to describe negative influences or traits, which seem to have a life and character of their own that pull against our wellbeing. For the early monks and nuns the appearance of demons enabled them to name and acknowledge what was destructive and so work to overcome it.

In the writings of the desert, the term 'demons' is used interchangeably with another term, *logosmoi*. *Logosmoi* are destructive trains of thought which invaded the heart and destroyed any chance of single-hearted devotion to God or a search for him. Consenting to evil thoughts implied a decision to collaborate with demons, a giving oneself over (on more levels of the self than the conscious person) to the powers of numbness lurking in the universe. But when willing to cooperate with angelic guides the monk or nun would find a renewal of faith and piety. So,

> Abba Anoub asked Abba Poemen about the impure thoughts which the heart of man brings forth and about vain desires. Abba Poemen said to him, 'Is the axe any use without someone to cut with it? (Is. 10.15) If you do not make use of these thoughts, they will be ineffectual too.' (Poemen 15)

This insight corresponds to what we know about the impact of rumination on our mental health. In fact the BBC Radio 4 programme *All in the Mind* launched a Stress Test in 2011, the biggest of its kind worldwide, which revealed that it is *how* we think about traumatic events in our lives that can significantly raise our stress levels. Two factors – rumination and self-blame – were identified as the most destructive ways of thinking about our difficulties. Rumination is a way of thinking about something that prolongs negative emotion. How one thinks about an event, especially one that has caused a negative emotional response in us, can shape the emotional response we have to it. Alternative routes to rumination are distraction, reappraisal or reframing. Abba Poemen's advice to stop thoughts in their tracks, combined with the understanding that trains of thought tend to the angelic or the demonic, can be a useful way of developing new perspectives on one's life.

### Praise the struggle

The *Sayings* reveal the importance of struggle and its need for growth and salvation. Although in pastoral situations to tell people that present difficulty is an opportunity for growth is crass and unhelpful, it is true that coming through well will involve struggle and will bring new strength. Thus pastors need to preach and teach in such a way as to point out the way in which struggle is part of ordinary human growth. We cannot avoid it but can meet it and, by understanding the processes, grow as human beings and as Christians. A church's culture can encourage people to deny their struggles or to pretend that they do not find embracing adversity a struggle because of their faith. At a basic level this makes it more difficult for people to survive serious illness, for example. Facing our demons involves naming and recognizing destructive influences and difficult events that have taken place in our lives. A pastor can assist by recognizing that life is complex and the influences of habits and experiences of the past stay with us. How we think about the past can change, however, but this will need courage and discipline. This is not to deny the experience of Christ in our lives, particularly when we first become Christians. It is a recognition that growing in the likeness and image of Christ is a process that begins in this life but continues beyond it. The biblical portrayal of the desert and the experience of the early desert Christians is that to face adversity and come through well will bring struggle that needs to be embraced, struggle of mind and of body.

## ADVICE THAT PROTECTS THE SELF

A self that is resourced and disciplined is needed to build resilience; a self undergirded by good enough self-esteem. Advice to disciples given by the desert elders focused on putting energy into growth, growth that will involve radical change.

The prominent themes in the *Sayings* related to self are to do with fleeing, sitting and guarding, directing energy within, and asceticism. These practices involve the whole person, body, mind and spirit, and they enable the disciple to embrace the desert – stage one of building resilience.

## Fleeing to and sitting with yourself

Desert Christians had heard the call to flee to the desert and away from their previous way of life. Thomas Merton describes the salvation sought by those who fled to the desert as a becoming of their true selves, unfettered by the constraints of social conformity, the aim being to have 'a clear unobstructed vision of the true state of affairs, an intuitive grasp of one's own inner reality as anchored, or rather lost, in God through Christ', the fruit of which is *quies*, or rest.[2] The monk was to become a truly integrated personality. To encounter the self involved fleeing from others to focus on growth:

> Abba Isaiah questioned Abba Macarius saying, 'Give me a word.' The old man said to him, 'Flee from people,' Abba Isaiah said to him, 'What does it mean to flee from people?' The old man said, 'It means to sit in your cell and weep for your sins.' (Macarius the Great 27)

There are times when we need to withdraw from particular relationships or even from most of them. Trauma, breakdown and serious illness often require us to flee and to sit in order to reassess where we are and plan for survival and wellbeing. That might mean leaving a job or a significant relationship, or fleeing a destructive way of life and seeking the refuge of a clinic to combat an addiction. It will certainly involve facing up to what is and mourning what has been lost.

Though entering the desert meant fleeing from a previous life, it did not mean running away from the self but facing the self, for the desert Christian sitting in the cell. The desert, both as a refuge from where you had come from and as a place of adversity, was somewhere where monks and nuns encountered themselves. This encounter with the self involved staying put, attending to the self and enduring emotional pain: 'A brother came to Scetis to visit Abba Moses and asked him for a word. The old man said to him, "Go, sit in your cell, and your cell will teach you everything"' (Moses 6). Amma Syncletia recommended that people should not constantly move around but instead attend to whatever had brought them to the desert to work on:

> If you find yourself in a monastery do not go to another place, for that will harm you a great deal. Just as the bird who abandons the eggs she was sitting on prevents them from hatching, so the monk or the nun grows cold and their faith dies, when they go from one place to another. (Syncletia 6)

Withdrawing and sitting with our stuff means we can begin to focus within, encounter our self and in doing so find strength to endure and to act.

### Guarding your inner self

Guarding the inner life and not judging are important features of desert spirituality. This is because healing and growing in Christian faith is life-giving and so necessary for a human being. To guard your inner life is to choose life and recognize that this requires directing your energy on life and healing and turning away from what depletes and destroys: 'Do not give your heart to that which does not satisfy your heart,' said Abba Poemen (Poemen 80).

There are various ways in which the *Sayings* describe ways of guarding the inner life. One is not judging yourself or others: 'A brother who shared a lodging with other brothers asked Abba Bessarion, "What should I do?" The old man replied, "Keep silence and do not compare yourself with others"' (Bessarion 10). 'Abba Macarius said, "If you reprove someone, you yourself get carried away by anger and you are satisfying your own passion; do not lose yourself, therefore, in order to save another"' (Macarius the Great 17). Non-judgement is a strategy for guarding and healing. Refusing to compare oneself with others and not judging enable energy to be directed towards growth.

Ascetic practices helped guard the inner life, by directing the disciple from the outside in. Fasting was commonly practised, as it still is in all the world's religious traditions, not to starve people but for its spiritual benefits. In Lent Christians are encouraged to fast and pray. Fasting assists mental alertness and prayer enables integration to come about: 'A brother asked Abba Tithoes, "How should I guard my heart?" The old man said to him, "How can we guard our hearts when our mouths and stomachs are open?"' (Tithoes 3). Fasting is recognized in the great spiritual traditions as increasing sensitivity to the non-material world, promoting mental alertness, enhancing personal experience of the sacredness of the self and the universe, and helping the person fasting to regain orientation and purpose and renew energy levels.

Fasting is not a popular practice among contemporary Christians, though we are familiar with our Muslim neighbours keeping Ramadan. Today people are more likely to use the language of detoxing and to understand the importance of diets that promote health in general than the language of fasting, though there is much shared understanding. We understand the need for diets to be tailored to specific individuals who need to reduce cholesterol, for example, or avoid gluten or take folic acid. These diets are fasts, even though we don't generally use that language. Fasting is hugely beneficial and I would make a plea for Christians to explore its spiritual benefits, just as we recognize there are more than physical benefits in giving up addictive substances, detoxing and following the diet the doctor recommends. For the desert Christians fasting at first restored the body to health and then kept the body in such a state as to enable the disciple to work on the inner person. Contemporary understandings of fasting affirm this, recognizing that the practice enables a person to focus within; rather than trying to escape the body it encourages a person to inhabit it. Fasting encourages a person to really hear, and respond, to the self, by consciously working with the fears raised by fasting by examining their roots.

The self-discipline of asceticism did not indicate neglecting or torturing the self. We guard our hearts and our energy by rest and relaxation as well as by discipline. St Antony was alone in a fortress for 20 years and yet we are told he emerged in glowing health. He allowed for relaxation and warned of the dangers of too strict a regime:

A hunter in the desert saw Abba Antony enjoying himself with the brethren and he was shocked. Wanting to show him that it was necessary sometimes to meet the needs of the brethren the old man said to him, 'Put an arrow in your bow and shoot it.' So he did. The old man then said, 'Shoot another,' and he did so. Then the old man said, 'Shoot yet again,' and the hunter replied 'If I bend my bow so much I will break it.' Then the old man said to him, 'It is the same with the work of God. If we stretch the brethren beyond measure they will soon break. Sometimes it is necessary to come down to meet their needs.' When he heard his words the hunter was pierced by compunction and, greatly edified by the old man, he went away. As for the brethren, they went home strengthened. (Antony 13)

Silence and solitude are also recommended ascetical practices which direct energy within and guard our inner lives in order that we may encounter the self and God. Refraining from speech enables the monk or nun to attend to the inner self. It was said of Abba Agathon that for three years he lived with a stone in his mouth, until he had learnt to keep silence (Agathon 15). 'The victory over all the afflictions that befall you, is, to keep silence' (Poemen 37).

## Resourcing the inner self

The inner life needs to be resourced as well as guarded. Desert Christians sought to maintain a constant sense of the divine presence in a meditative state which was nourished by prayer, manual labour, fasting and psalmody. Egyptian monasticism practised a continuous psalmody, interspersed with prayer and sustained for extended periods of time in an effort to maintain a state of meditation.

For John Cassian the programme of growth begins with the desire to respond to a call to seek the kingdom of God by pursuing the monastic virtue of purity of heart. A vision of an attainable future enabled the monk to be motivated to grow and have hope. We have seen how important the hope of a future is for children, teenagers and adults experiencing adversity that will not pass quickly and so must be endured. The biblical language of promise and a vision of the future provides the fuel by which people can endure. The concept of purity of heart in Cassian is a concept which enabled the monks to endure adversity. Purity of heart is not a fixed concept but can also be described as holiness, perfection, contemplation, spiritual knowledge and love. Cassian recommends that purity of heart must be pursued by the most direct route. What the *Sayings* and Cassian recommend is what writers on resilience observe – energy must be put into the call to love, and as a priority. For Cassian, whatever directs the monk to the goal is to be pursued with all his strength, and whatever deters the monk is to be avoided as dangerous and harmful. In fact, whatever disturbs the purity and tranquillity of the mind, however useful and necessary it may appear to be, must be avoided as harmful. For Cassian the call of the monk to perfection, freedom and love through the struggle of self-discipline must come above everything else. This is particularly so because purity of heart is progressive and includes the possibility of diminishment or loss. The Benedictine theologian Columba Stewart describes purity of heart in Cassian, not as a trait of the untested where a pristine state must be protected from corruption, but as a trait of human beings who are fully alive despite and because of the scars inevitably left by this life. Stewart argues that all the descriptions of the experience of Christian perfection by Cassian suggest it is a focusing of fragmented energies on what is truly important.[3] Concepts like purity of heart and perfection, understood as a focus and direction of energy rather than a static and unattainable state, provide the Christian with a path to building resilience.

## Pastoral ministry and the resilient self

The life and teachings of the desert Christians were directed towards loving God; that involved knowing themselves, recognizing who they were before God and growing towards God. In their example we have a pattern of life, ancient in the Christian tradition, that reveals the priorities needed for people who are faced with adversity and need to make radical changes in their lives – physical, mental, emotional and spiritual. Resilience literature describes this process of strengthening by the 3 Cs of *Coping, Constancy* and *Construction*; and the initial facing of adversity and embracing of the desert involves coping and being constant in the face of destruction or diminishment. This is done by fleeing, sitting, guarding, resourcing and discipline and involves the whole person. As pastors we must take care not to discount the spiritual dimensions and benefits that accompany people who make changes in their lives when adversity strikes; whether it be taking up a diet, exercise, or giving up bad habits of any sort.

To help people to embrace the desert, to embark on the changes needed to meet the challenge that illness, for example, has brought, pastors need to affirm a self-focus. This can be difficult if the Christian culture tends towards emphasizing the idea that any focus on the self is selfish and the way to holiness is through self-denial and self-sacrifice. Adversity threatens the self and so an engagement with one's situation and attention to one's inner life is necessary to find the self-esteem and worth necessary to struggle, as is having a sense of the future. For the pastor, preaching and teaching as well as providing material for individuals should resource people with a vision of abundant life, stories of Christians or saints who inspire and prayers that can articulate trust and hope. These can help people to build a self-esteem rooted in the experience and knowledge of God's love which strengthens them. To encourage a self-focus is not to encourage self-blame or comparing oneself with others. Pastors need to be conscious that in sharing stories of Christians coming through adversities with God's help they must not cause people to lose heart because they are not 'doing as well'. Such accounts need to be truthful and witness to the way in which strengthening comes through struggle and support. Pastors need consciously not to judge, but instead respect the diverse ways in which people approach difficulty. They need to support a resilience process, not set out an impossible route.

To take up something new – and meeting the challenge of adversity is taking up something new – means laying down other things. Pastors can give people permission to say no, to be alone, to be silent and reflective, to flee or not be in touch with people who will not be supportive. The purpose of this kind of protecting the self is that energy can be directed to coping and being constant, and it involves the whole person, including the physical. It doesn't mean leaving people alone, but showing your availability and support regularly and without interfering. Pastors can encourage people to be self-disciplined in those things that promote their health – physical, emotional and spiritual. This is recommending embracing the path of asceticism for the purposes of healing and growth, however much we wish it were not necessary. It was bereavement that sent St Antony on the ascetic life, persecution that sent Hagar and Moses. Adversity requires change, often radical change, of lifestyle and perspective. Adversity involves being denied the things that give pleasure; adversity brings austerity of life – these things are true for a widow, for example, or a teenager whose parents are divorcing. What the concept of asceticism adds to adversity is the perspective: adversity is used by ascetics in order to grow, to mature, to pursue love, to search for God. What an ascetic chooses to use – a strict diet, time alone – is forced on many people awaiting or recovering from surgery. We might encourage those facing difficulty by understanding how these difficulties might bring about wellbeing of body, mind and spirit.

## PURSUING AUTHENTIC RELATIONSHIPS

Desert Christians fled the world and the relationships that went with living in the world. Fleeing from the world, and for the most part even from family, can give the sense that, for the desert Christians, relationships were to be shunned. However, the variety of lives that we now know ascetics of the time led – at home and in towns, as well as in the desert – reveals a metaphorical dimension to flight. The desert Christians provide a model of healthy relating, shown in the advice to flee from destructive relationships as well as in the nature of the relationship between the elder and the disciple. We find in the *Sayings* the recognition of the need to put energy into authentic relationships and withdraw from some for the sake of one's wellbeing: 'Restrain yourself from affection towards many people, for fear lest your spirit be distracted, so that your interior peace may not be disturbed' (Evagrius 2).
    Though a disciple fled to the desert, even fled from destructive

elationships, it was understood in the desert tradition that no one entered the desert alone and no one could grow towards perfection alone. Relationships with other people were necessary for the desert Christians, not least because of the difficulties of surviving in the desert. The way of life was determined by the concrete social relations that reflected continued economic dependence on the settled world for food.

## The elder and disciple relationship

The disciple in the desert always had a relationship with an elder because the beginner did not possess the discernment necessary to assess his or her own personal progress. The basis of the relationship was absolute obedience owed by the disciple to the elder, something we are appropriately wary of today because of the opportunities for a person in an authoritative position to abuse that power. The disciple was to have complete trust, which was the basis of the obedience, and the elder had to use the gift of spiritual discernment to adapt his or her advice to the needs and capacities of the disciple. The *Sayings* are the witness of this relationship where what is said is direct and pertinent to the needs of an individual.

A central practice was that of 'manifesting one's thoughts' to the elder. This was done because the disciple could only gradually learn to discern his own thoughts. Not to share one's thoughts but instead try to direct oneself in the ascetic life indicated self-deception and a temptation to self-reliance. Manifesting thoughts was an indication of growth in humility, which is seeing the self as God sees:

A brother asked Abba Poemen, 'Why should I not be free to do without manifesting my thoughts to the old men?' The old man replied, 'Abba John the Dwarf said, "The enemy rejoices over nothing so much as over those who do not manifest their thoughts."' (Poemen 101)

A monk or nun had only one abba or amma, and did not continually discuss his or her spiritual state. Disciples manifesting their thoughts were confident enough in God's mercy, working through the elder, to turn the soul inside out without cleaning it all up beforehand. This needed trust, and to share one's thoughts, rather than ruminating over events, prevented destructive thoughts from having a chance to lodge themselves into a chamber of the inner self and grow twisted and perverse. Demons were shown to have only illusory power which manifesting thoughts exposed. Non-judgement and humility characterized the relationship in both directions, inviting not a soft love, but a relating with discernment for both oneself and the other.[4] An elder was the person who through support and wisdom enabled the disciple to embrace the desert and by following the way of life encounter God by self-discipline and the life of prayer and so grow in love and holiness.

John Cassian provides an astute understanding of being a pastor and, although he does not describe it in such terms, the need for any pastor to be on the journey of resilience. The third stage of the desert metaphor reveals that in the process of growth through adversity altruism emerges; and this, surely, should be a characteristic of the pastoral relationship. Those who have suffered often end up in pastoral ministry. Altruistic activity, as this third stage of a resilience process, can in Cassian take the form of becoming an abba or an amma. Mentoring – as an elder – is a key component of Cassian's model of growth: it is a form of altruistic activity requiring empathy, compassion and discernment. The wise monk is sought out by disciples to guide them. Such a ministry of teaching and counsel often became part of the vocation even of solitaries. We see this in the life of Antony, famous as a solitary, but described frequently as involved with mentoring monks and even as taking part in politics.

Cassian describes the desert elder as a witness and encourager who gave very little or no advice. The qualities required were of availability and patience: not direction, but being present to or accompanying another person. Desert elders recognized themselves in their disciples who were troubled, and they acted out of their experience that compassion in solidarity was the only way forward. Not out to control, the elder was to assist disciples in opening themselves up to others and to God. Elders were sometimes called healers although they were more of a witness or a

midwife whose qualification was the experience of seeing themselves as sinners and accepting that it was only God's mercy that
could bring hope and forgiveness, along with their own hard work.

Discernment was the key quality of an elder. It is required in
order to judge how much adversity will strengthen, rather than
crush, a person. Cassian prescribes just enough adversity to bring
about self-awareness. Discernment, discretion or wisdom is the
quality an elder needs to be of help to a disciple, and it was considered to be a gift of God's grace, sought with utter humility and
attentiveness to self.

## THE PASTORAL RELATIONSHIP

Much of the description of the elder–disciple relationship rings
true for good pastoral care. The *Sayings* themselves provide a good
pastoral model – brief, appropriate affirmation and challenge for a
specific time and place, in the context of a relationship of trust and
openness. Little is said about prayer in the *Sayings* and there is no
theological discussion. People in adversity do not need a teacher,
but someone to accompany them in responding to the call to take
up the struggle of the adversity of the desert. When someone is
facing adversity, on the brink of embracing the desert and then
adjusting to its landscape, pithy sayings, appropriate to the state
of mind and heart of the hearer, can provide encouragement and
strength. For words to be appropriate they need to emerge in the
context of the pastoral relationship – from the ability of the pastor
to be present with someone suffering and to empathize.

The quality of discernment or wisdom, the ability to say the
right thing, comes today, as it did in the days of the desert Christians, from the experience of having 'been there' and come through
so as to be strengthened. That the pastor has been made strong
and is resilient is expressed in pastoral ministry by humility and
wisdom.

Pastors may not think that they have much power, but they do.
That is why humility – the knowledge that you are human too and
need help from other people and God – is so important. Certainly
there is not the expectation that a member of the congregation
today will obey the advice given by the pastor, but pastors do have

power and influence over people and need to acknowledge this in order not to abuse it. It is not the 'manifestation of thoughts' that pastors hear today, but formally and informally they are party to the thoughts and feelings of people's lives. Resilient people are those who have been able to exercise autonomy, especially at times when they have little control over their lives. Thus advice giving is less likely to enable people to find strength than listening to them and conveying that whatever is said will not be judged. A discerning pastor can spot destructive cycles of self-blame and doubt as well as a lack of honesty and, like a good counsellor, by listening and support discern ways to help people face the truth of their situation.

## Identity and the pastor

For Cassian, it is not altruism that is the transformative power in enabling resilience, but the grace of God. Altruism cannot save the individual, nor can it save the world; such salvation is achieved by what God has done in Christ. Thus, for Cassian, pastors must be aware that they cannot solve the problems of an individual or the world. It is with humility that they will be able to recognize God's role in human lives.

The human effort made towards the healing of the self by asceticism, and of the world by altruism, are insufficient to achieve their purpose and will come to an end, as Cassian points out. Both works of asceticism and of service are provisional, though they are essential in the present life. Practical work bears many fruits, but because of such variety in expression it cannot compare to the single focus of contemplation. The process of resilience described in resilience literature ends with the resilient being altruistic people, ones who show compassion, humility and wisdom, but who continue to struggle within themselves, for one can never fully heal one's hurts. For Cassian, the practical life will cease after death so that works of mercy, though necessary now, he argues, are not essential to human nature; there will be a time beyond them. For Cassian, service of others or ministry, as well as the struggle of asceticism, will end; but love or contemplation in purity of heart will remain. Not only does Cassian's model, then, take us beyond the resilience process described in studies of the resilient, but it has implications for those who are involved in altruistic activity and experience healing through it. Cassian issues a challenge to pastors and how they see themselves. Pastoral work is but a means to an end, and this means that one's self-understanding in terms of identity and practice cannot reside in being a pastor. This is a profound challenge to those of us who see ourselves as pastors. Pastoral work will come to an end. In the kingdom of God, there will be no need for pastors to help people in adversity, for there will be no adversity. Pastors, like the emergency services, will be redundant. And so our identity needs to be rooted more deeply in our baptism and in our discipleship than in our understanding of ourselves as pastors. We must ask ourselves what drives us and what the dynamics of healing and helping are in our own history and ministry.

## Acedia, the vice of the pastor

Cassian is famous for his writing on vice. Struggle brings growth in the form of pursuing virtue. The last eight of the 12 books of the *Institutes*, the full title of which is *The Institutes of the Cenobites, and the Remedies for the Eight Principal Vices*, as well as Conference Five, are devoted to a consideration of the eight vices. Each book of the *Institutes* introduces a vice as a struggle or a conflict: gluttony, fornication, avarice, anger, sadness, acedia, vainglory and pride, with the remedies for uprooting them. The order of battle for Cassian is from the most carnal of the vices to the most spiritual, with gluttony taking first place and pride last, described as the most spiritual, an inwardly nourished vice.

It is the vice of acedia that is the downfall of the pastor. Cassian provides insightful observations about the pastor's vice – better described as acedia (or sometimes accidie) rather than sloth. Acedia is the vice that draws pastors away from their own growth in holiness, resulting in a sense of superiority and poor pastoral practice. Pope Gregory the Great (d. 604) reduced Cassian's eight vices into seven capital vices – later to become the seven deadly sins – and in this change acedia was lost.

Acedia, or the vice of sloth, has been notoriously difficult to define. Described as the Noonday Demon of Psalm 91 (v. 6), it manifests itself among other things in sleeping in the afternoon.

Acedia has traditionally been understood as the sin of sloth or the ancient depiction of a variety of psychological states and behaviours such as laziness, ennui or boredom. It has been considered to be analogous to the modern clinical condition of depression and professional burnout syndrome. More helpful contemporary understandings of acedia reveal it to be of most value for self-awareness in the pastor. Acedia was the vice removed by Gregory the Great in the sixth century, but it has been given attention today by spiritual writers. It functions as the vice for which resilience is the virtue and as such addresses the themes of struggle, self and relationships. The spiritual writer Kathleen Norris describes acedia as an absence of care for the self, a kind of spiritual morphine where a person knows that pain is present but doesn't care, being too passive to cry out. Abbot Christopher Jamison describes acedia as spiritual apathy or spiritual carelessness, arguing that there is a great need for self-awareness in contemporary culture.

The demon of acedia shows itself by physical as well as psychological effects, which are detailed by Cassian but come from an older and broader tradition. A saying of Amma Theodora, for example, states:

> You should realise that as soon as you intend to live in peace, at once evil comes and weighs down your soul through acedia, faintheartedness, and evil thoughts. It also attacks your body through sickness, debility, weakening of the knees, and all the members. It dissipates the strength of soul and body, so that one believes one is ill and no longer able to pray. (Theodora 3)

Cassian describes acedia as a wearied or anxious heart which is akin to sadness and the peculiar lot of solitaries. It comes on like a fever at the sixth hour and makes a person feel horrified at where he is, disgusted with his cell and also disdainful and contemptuous of the brothers. Rendering him slothful and immobile with regard to work, it does not allow him to stay still in his cell or devote any efforts to reading. The monk feels he will possess no spiritual fruit attached to this group of people and makes a great deal of far off and distant monasteries. When the spirit is worn out by acedia, agitated as by the most powerful battering ram, there are two courses of action. One is to succumb to sleep and the other is to find consolation by visiting a brother. Overcome with acedia the monk stays in his cell without any spiritual progress, or else is driven from his cell in a way that is unstable or feckless and becomes trapped in the affairs, harmful concerns and business of others. He can undertake apparently virtuous activities, such as charitable work and caring for the sick, but to the wrong measure and with the wrong motivation. The monk in this condition is in danger of using other people in order to feel good about himself, rather than remain in his cell making no spiritual progress. Acedia expresses itself as both self-denigration and a superiority which is critical of the failings of others. The monk believes that the community has become unspiritual and does not provide the necessary support that he needs because others are no longer compassionate and there is no one to console him. Thus the effects of acedia can be seen in those who are slothful as well as those who are busy. The most consistent advice given to the monk affected is not to leave his cell.

It seems to be that Christian pastors can succumb to laziness – not taking their pastoral responsibilities seriously but avoiding or neglecting them. Christian pastors can succumb to being busybodies, dependent for their self-worth on helping others. Both expressions of acedia can go with resentment of others and one's ministry and lead to a kind of sneering, superior attitude towards other Christians. For Cassian, it is the virtue of fortitude or courage that 'will begin to cultivate what acedia was laying waste'. I suggest that today we would call it resilience; and pursuing resilience counteracts the damage caused by acedia. Acedia is a lack of care, a refusal to struggle and to grow which manifests itself in sleep, inaction or else in activity, such as pastoral work, in order to avoid dealing with the inner self. A reading of the vice of acedia through the resilience themes of struggle, self and relationships points to a state of mind where the motivation for growth is lacking, and which is allied to a lack of self-awareness and self-care. This results in avoiding facing oneself and one's situation and the emotional pain that goes with it. Sleep provides the opportunity to avoid oneself, and so does visiting other people. This vice is particularly pertinent to those who have a vocation to pastoral ministry. Visiting gives pastors a sense of superiority and control because by witnessing the difficulties of others they can seemingly be of service to them and thus feel morally good about themselves. In addition, having avoided the struggle inevitable in growth and development, the pastors are less aware of their own vulnerabilities and complex feelings and so can delude themselves about their superiority in coping with life over and against those whom they visit. This results in poor if not exploitative pastoral practice, and leads us to the dangers associated with the model of the wounded healer which we shall explore in Chapter 6.

**Summary**

The lives and teaching of the desert Christians affirm the three movements of the desert metaphor as a resilience process. The *Sayings* particularly address the need to embrace the desert by flight, staying, guarding and resourcing the inner self. Cassian's writings challenge the resilient to look beyond altruism as the source of healing. Healing and peace, however, are not found in one's identity as an elder or pastor. Cassian challenges Christian pastors not to seek their identity in helping others nor to think they can save the world. Such attributes are liable to feed the vice of acedia which works against resilience. Cassian's presentation of acedia provides those called to pastoral ministry with an understanding of the snares of work carried out without the struggle to be motivated, attention to self and self-care, and humility before others and God. A pastor who brings about healing and strength in the lives of those in adversity is a pastor who seeks to grow. This means avoiding the vice of acedia and struggling to develop the virtue of resilience through disciplined attention to self, making use of the resources available and the help of others.

# CHAPTER FIVE

# Rowan Williams and resilient believing

## THE CONVERSATION SO FAR

The time has now come to gather the threads of the conversation we have been having to discover what will best help strengthen people in adversity and so shape a pastoral theology of resilience. Studies in resilience have shown us that someone open to change, fuelled by an inner life and vision of the future, and able to exercise self-discipline is well placed to be motivated to take up struggle with adversity and come through strengthened. Having relationships that encourage, support and respect autonomy is significant in making the journey from adversity to a life where growth continues to take place, expressed by altruistic living. The conversation with the Bible's portrayal of the desert experience confirms the themes of studies in resilience and enables us to see the journey of being strengthened in adversity as one marked by three stages: embracing the desert, encountering one's self and God, and altruistic living, which involves pastoral responsibility. Desert Christians who drew inspiration from the landscape and spirituality of the desert echo the need to flee from what is destructive and draining and put energy into embracing the desert and, by the discipline of asceticism, face demons and seek growth in virtue. The themes of an inner life and vision of the future enable strengthening to take place, as does a relationship with a wise elder to guide.

There are, however, loose ends in this conversation. We need to have a Christian theological understanding of struggle, self and relationships for our own time. It is all very well to draw on the richness of early desert spirituality, but we need to consider carefully the application of its wisdom for today. We cannot commend the monastic virtues of obedience, self-denial and humility without thought, and we need to take account of where there is neglect of the body and relationships in the monastic tradition. Studies in resilience warn against the way in which these Christian concepts have played themselves out negatively in the lives of people struggling with adversity. Pastors are all too aware of these issues – such as the way in which some people are only too willing to submit to God's will if it looks like a quick and easy solution and means any struggling with deeper issues can be avoided. For some, an aspiration to humility plays into low self-esteem and faith is lived out as fatalistic passivity, rather than providing motivation to struggle and be strengthened to come through. We need a contemporary Christian understanding of the desert tradition if we are to use it to help people make sense of their experience of adversity and enable them to be strengthened through it, and if we are to meet the challenges to Christian faith and practice that the studies in resilience present.

## ROWAN WILLIAMS IN CONVERSATION WITH RESILIENCE AND THE DESERT TRADITION

Rowan Williams, academic theologian and Archbishop of Canterbury, has been a prolific theological author over several decades. He has written on many subjects which reveal common ground between early Christian and contemporary theologies of resilience. Williams writes in dialogue with the monastic tradition of the desert, psychotherapy and contemporary understandings of self, and has been able to address these not only in academic and professional circles but in the context of spirituality and action. Such a conversation partner is necessary to draw on the richness of the Christian tradition of desert experience and literature of the past and present a coherent contemporary theology of struggle, self and relationships which can contribute to a pastoral theology of resilience.

This chapter will show how Williams explores the themes of struggle, self and relationships which are interwoven in his theology, and how he reinterprets the monastic tradition. Williams also attends to the process of struggling to grow as one that is expressed in altruism. He points to the importance of attention, hesitation and contemplation as a means of being strengthened in adversity, not only personally, but in such a way as to contribute to the formation of community and society.

## THE IMPORTANCE OF STRUGGLE

Struggle as a means of growth is a prominent theme in Rowan Williams's theology. The struggle is not with God. The struggle is with oneself in order to become self-aware and to grow, to deepen and to love. In addressing what Rowan Williams says about the understanding of the place of struggle in strengthening and growth three aspects are particularly important:

- his reinterpretation of the monastic struggle for contemporary Christians;
- the struggle and frustrations that heighten self-consciousness, particularly in a therapeutic relationship;
- the deepening of pain and struggle through trust and obedience, which brings a new capacity for love after the pattern of Christ and Christian mystics such as St John of the Cross.

Williams has written on monasticism as an academic theologian and reinterpreted the tradition more popularly for Christian audiences.[1] In itself the monastic profession does not achieve anything, Williams argues, but it provides a stable geographical and psychological setting where the important battles may be fought. Growth comes through conflict, and to acknowledge such is realistic and a warning against complacency and a static, self-oriented spiritual life. Williams recognizes the problematic element in describing the Christian life as a battle, for an emphasis on effort and vigilance can seem neurotic and lay itself open to a spirituality of what Freud called the super ego, with its critical and moralizing role. But for the desert Christians, it is the profound acceptance of failure as part of human life that means Williams points to the monasticism of that time as being on the side of grace.

Struggle is necessary for growth, in the monastic life and for us today. The struggle is with ourselves, not with God. We prefer not to look inside at our inner confusion because it is painful to do so. What needs addressing is how hard we find it to make space for anyone else or for God. Williams interprets the monastic discipline of staying in the cell as fundamentally staying in touch with the reality of being human – a limited creature who is not in control of everything and is an unfinished being in the hands of the maker.

Williams acknowledges the painfulness of struggling with the self, describing it as feeling like hell most of the time, but it is necessary to be able to love. The monastic tradition uses strong language and the concepts of dying to self and self-denial need to be understood carefully. Williams describes dying to the self as putting on hold and letting go of one's own perspective for the sake of another, because it is in solidarity with one's neighbour that life is found. Being 'dead to your neighbour' means freeing your neighbour from your judgements and instead loving the person actually present to you, not trying to make that person into the one you would want. Attention to one's own turmoil – which includes self-awareness and self-worth – is necessary for loving others. Inattention to one's own struggle can block someone else's relation with Christ, because then you can be harsh and quick to judge and prescribe and fail to respond to that person's needs.

Self-denial is not a virtue to pursue for its own sake, nor for a competition with others, but a device to aid attentiveness to the self and others. Williams points to the need to hold being strenuous and relaxed in tension. We need to be strenuous in the effort to keep before our eyes the truth of our condition, and be relaxed as we recognize God's mercy that can never be exhausted. That the desert monks and nuns have varying attitudes to physical self-denial shows that different people need different disciplines to keep them attentive.

So the desert tradition, Williams argues, recognizes the reality of struggle for growth in self-awareness and discipline and the necessity of these for love. Dying to ourselves and self-denial are painful, but these ascetic practices have the aim of enabling attention to be focused on someone else and on God, on growth, not for their own sake. These principles are as relevant today as then, though they are experienced in other contexts in contemporary life, such as therapy.

## Struggles that heighten self-consciousness

It is not only by monastic discipline and denial that growth is enabled. The struggles and frustrations that heighten self-consciousness in ordinary life lead to growth. Williams identifies the experience of frustrated desire as a moment of growth which belongs to the essence of development itself. When we experience a gap between desire and reality, what we are and what we want, and we do not just react, we are consolidating the self. A reaction comes quickly and without thought. When there is a moment of self-questioning and a refusal to evade pain and shock, a pause, we can bring about soul by the process of attending to the moment. Thus we respond rather than react. Williams describes holding on to the difficulty as the beginning of authentic religious practice. Frustrated desire is part of ordinary living, but it can also be planned – through ascetical practices such as fasting or celibacy. Planned frustration is also found in therapy.

In therapy, opportunities for frustration can occur in the experience of the analytical relationship, for the therapist does not provide answers and advice. When 'transference' occurs the client experiences the analyst as refusing to ratify or reveal the answer to his or her desire. The client can then perhaps begin to understand what a self is and what it isn't. The self is what is coming to birth in the process of experiencing frustrated desire. An analyst must, of course, resist the seductive pressure to become necessary and be persistently aware of his or her own frustrated desire in not meeting the desire of the client. The presence of another person enables the self to mature and be truthful, that is if the analyst is not meeting needs or providing answers to otherness, to God.[2]

## The deepening of pain and struggle

The deepening of pain and struggle through trust and obedience is a further aspect of Williams's exploration of the place of struggle in growth. This deepening is after the pattern of Christ crucified.

Christ's example, as Williams describes it, is not a journey towards a kind of peace that is passive. Williams warns against seeking a kind of peace that means not acting or not having to choose or involve one's self, for that is really longing for an infantile condition where nothing happens. The peace that Jesus creates between God and the world is not a tepid coexistence or non-interference. To be drawn into Christ's peace, for Williams, means entering into Christ's space and so bearing, as he did, the tensions of knowing the full force of hope and grief.

Williams points to Jesus' obedience in the circumstances of his earthly life, in temptation and fear, as what opens the long-closed door between God and human hearts. The obedience of Jesus, he says, is the attitude of alert attention, the giving up of his life moment by moment to his Father, not in bland passivity, but taken, seen, probed and responded to. Jesus sees the Father, sees directly, unwaveringly even, in terror and death, and his trust in the Father is manifest alike in authority and vulnerability, dependence as well as humility, responsiveness and receptivity.[3]

This journey is one that each human being must make. Each must 'obey Christ, surrender to the pattern of his sacrificial torment and death – not in some kind of constructed self immolation, but in response to the trials encountered simply in living as a believer, living in the insecurities of faith, the conviction of things not seen'. The growth is brought about by deepening pain which involves anguish and darkness and obedient acceptance of God's will. It is only by trust and obedience that we can make the journey. We go to Christ beyond 'the settled and the ordered, to the place where Jesus died in his night, his desert'.[4]

This process is continuous for Christians, for whom growth in conflict is a constant experience. In this fire we are healed and restored, but we are not taken out of it. The experience of pain being deepened enables a person to identify with others experiencing pain and struggling and so develop empathy. In suffering, the believer's self-protection and isolation are broken: the heart is broken so as to make space for others and for compassion. This new capacity for love displaces the ego which enables space for others. Believers are called to exercise freedom, to create their lives in the arena of moral struggle, temptation and uncertainty, and this is a vocation requiring trust, courage and a readiness to confront the wilderness that lies ahead.[5]

Williams writes in his book *The Wound of Knowledge* about the experience of St John of the Cross, who accepts the fact that there is a draining and crucifying conflict at the centre of Christian living and refuses to countenance any joy or celebration which has not faced this conflict and endured it. Williams points to St John of the Cross, Martin Luther and other great writers of the Christian past who see the test of integrity as whether a man or woman has lived in the central darkness of the Christian story, whether they have known why it is that God is killed by his creatures and their religion, and how God himself breaks and reshapes all religious language as he acts through vulnerability, failure and contradiction.

In discussing the spirituality of St John of the Cross, Williams discusses the experience of the dark night of the soul. This involves an acute sense of rejection, humiliation and worthlessness, a sort of dissolution of the sense of self, which St John claims is the necessary prelude to union with God and the final siege of self-defence and self-reliance. Williams points out that this is not a technique of self-abasement but the felt consequences of developing closeness with God. It is difficult, he says, to separate the knowledge given in the experience of the night from the intense emotional accompaniments of self-loathing, fear and confusion, the sense of abandonment by God, of condemnation to hell. Though St John describes the experience as rare, Williams suggests it is not uncommon and that its character is central to the enterprise of faith itself. Alienation and dread are produced by all kinds of experiences, he comments, including the frustrations and humiliations of daily life, all of which are intrinsic to this experience of a sense of the lack of God and being aware of one's own wretchedness. The experience serves as a preparation for the authentic union of the self with God, which involves direct and joyful experience of God, reciprocal love and a fresh sense of the world as God's world.[6]

## THE SELF AND THE SOUL

Studies in resilience emphasize the importance of knowing oneself to be of value, of having a future and of being self-disciplined in order to deal with adversity and come through strengthened. The studies also recognize that the need for self-reliance in many of the resilient when they were in difficult circumstances can be hard to shed and makes it difficult for them to trust and form intimate relationships. Williams's theology addresses who we are in relationship to each other and to God. Here our vulnerability, the riskiness of life and of relating are what it means to be human – with trust, accompanied by humility and contemplation, the only creative option as our selves grow into souls.

### The self formed in relationship to God: creatureliness

The doctrine of creation is a statement that everything depends on the action of God: human beings are creatures, and there is absolute difference between the creator and the world. Creation is the utterance and overflow of divine life as self-love and self-gift, for God desires us and to be here is to be of God because God wants it so. Our humanity is not functional to any purpose of God, for God is without need and so there is a possibility of freedom and security for the self. Humanity does not need to struggle against God for its welfare and interests. Human beings, however, are averse to their own creatureliness and are strongly attracted to the 'illusion of omnipotence' or at least of being an individual, self-regulating system. Dependence is inevitable for a human being, but so is the need to be an agent who is not confined by dependence. Williams describes the forming of human identity in the metaphor of language: God summons in creation, and human beings form through conversation. The conversation begins at birth and is one where we receive before we give and give only as a response to receiving. It is as givers that we are agents and need to know that we exist for another 'in relation, conversation, mutual recognition', not as a self-regulating individual. Such dependence on others as we form our identity is risky because we may fall victim to exploitation by those who seek to shore up their identities over and against us.

Thus the choice is to negotiate our identity fearfully or trust in our capacity to give. Williams recommends trust in God, for 'with God alone, I am dealing with what does not need to construct or negotiate an identity, what is free to be itself without the process of struggle'.[7]

The decision to trust in God, to have faith, begins in the experience of alienation from self, of adversity and self-awareness. As creatures we must grow into what we are and there is always the possibility of failing to grow as we should. A true coming to oneself involves humility, a recognition of total poverty and an accepting of limit and death. As creatures, growth and fullness come by contemplation. Creation is there because of the limitless capacity of God for contemplation, for allowing the other to be. Contemplation for human beings means taking the risk of trusting God, and in gratitude and silence waiting on God without clear prediction or security. Contemplation is demanding, involving a stripping and letting the self be clothed in Christ, moulded by what is other. To contemplate God 'is among other things the struggle to become the kind of person who can without fear be open to divine activity'.[8]

Our bodies are important. When human beings contemplate God they do so as embodied spirits. Williams reinterprets the monastic tradition for contemporary life by describing the body as simply the place where we know we shall meet God. The inner life, he says, is not capable of transforming itself for it is 'only the body that saves the soul'. Staying in the cell, then, is a pledging of the body for the body is the place, the furnace, where the Son of God walks.[9] Prayer and contemplation enable human beings to learn to attend to their bodies and be conscious of how they inform the desire and openness of prayer. Williams points to the Eastern Christian's technique of observing the rhythms of the body, breathing and heartbeat, as part of becoming aware of material creatureliness, not to control it, but to come to terms with our lives and our memories and be at peace with ourselves. For Williams salvation is in no sense a flight to God from what is human, but is the realizing of God's likeness and so the sharing of his life in what is human. To see the proper goal of spirituality as the overcoming of human nature is highly problematic, Williams argues. Human growth is becoming more yourself, and thus the Church should be faithful to its basic task of telling people that a willingness to be who they are, and to begin to change only from the point of that recognition, is fundamental in the encounter with God. The desert, Williams declares, is a place where you go to become more particular than ever.

## The self formed in relationship to others: the soul

Williams develops his idea of selfhood as emerging soul, formed in relation to others and as one tells the story of one's life, in his book *Lost Icons*, which he describes as an essay about the erosions of selfhood in North Atlantic modernity. For Williams, the use of the term 'soul' presupposes relationships as the ground that gives the self room to exist. In the first place, God, as agent, addresses or summons the self as an act, not of need but of gift. The soul is not an immaterial individual substance but an integrity one struggles to bring into existence over time. For soul to emerge, more than an inner life is needed because a well-developed inner life could seek invulnerability rather than being answerable to the perceptions of others. The self forms in conversation and soul emerges in telling the story of one's life, and is shaped by every retelling. In telling the stories of our lives we realize we are not in control of our own stories: they do not belong exclusively to us since actions have effects and meanings we did not foresee or intend. Such a realization brings with it the acknowledgement that we are incomplete and that to become our real selves means being involved in the continuing and risky process of relating. A person seeks for home and the search ends when it reaches God, who is not a place of comfortable self-sufficiency, but an arena of unending new discovery, reappraisal and fresh vision. A self that can be called a soul exists in the expectation of God's grace, which is possible when we know that we are loved, significant and wanted, for then we can let go of our defences and trust God.

Awareness of the story of one's life and the ways in which it has been shaped by others reveals feelings of remorse, shame and injury, as well as honour. Remorse is a prominent theme in Williams's understanding of how soul is formed in relationship to others. Remorse involves thinking and imagining one's identity and the ways in which one has become part of the self-representation of others, both individuals and groups. It is the recognition of a loss already experienced by oneself and another. This recognition involves a loss of control and power and is part of the realization that a person forms, not as the result of a neutral and natural process, but as the deposit of choices, accidents and risks. We cannot love ourselves truthfully or absolve ourselves without the love and investment of others.

Fullness of life is a collaborative process and 'there is nothing good for one that is not good for both, nothing bad for one that is not bad for both'.[10] One can resist growing or forming as a soul by seeking a static and defended sense of self closed to the perceptions of others. Therapy, Williams argues, can be used as a tool of denial and a way of neutralizing the perspectives of others by retreating into an enclosed frame of reference where the story of victimization becomes a total explanation or justification for all the contours of a biography. Williams argues that therapy should not serve the purpose of creating or restoring a sense of solitary peace with oneself. As injuries from formative years are brought to light, healing will require challenging the person responsible to accept the effects of their actions or habits of the past. What is due to victims is, in fact, to be part of the conversation and so to have the freedom to share in the definition of who and what they are. A silenced self is a sign of another's guilt and oppression – a situation where people don't talk to each other but describe other people's experience in their own language. A new type of conversation takes time and is always an unfinished task with misstatement and misrecognition common from both sides. The traditional religious concept of repentance Williams describes as intimately bound up with the hope of change and particularly changed relationships. Forgiveness seeks to create new solidarity but is not to be confused with leniency or making light of an outrage – thus its achievement matters less than the indication of hope and the need for the lost connection that seeking forgiveness represents.

## RELATIONSHIPS AND COMMUNITY

As is already clear, for Williams the self is formed in relationship. Finding one's own life is a task that cannot be undertaken without the neighbour, for life itself is what we find in solidarity. Relationships are what Christ's healing ministry restored in order to form the body of Christ, the Church. The process of salvation is flesh becoming body, just as we have noted that self becomes soul. It is not only therapeutic relationships that enable self-awareness and growth, but also the experience of being in love. Williams explores the dynamics of human relating with listening, attention and freedom given as characteristic of healthy relationships. He also stresses the need for Christians to resist what is oppressive. Pastoral relationships require mutual growth with attention to human experience and the life of Christ.

Williams draws on St Paul's use of the term 'flesh' as describing human life without relationships, as empty, untenanted life, where there is no spark to relate. Flesh is that system of destructive reactions and instincts that keeps us prisoners to sin, with the flesh used in a meaningless, destructive or isolating way, putting a ceiling on our growth towards God. God's grace makes flesh inhabited by spirit so that it becomes a language, a system, a means of connection. Human stories told as love stories or through the arts reveal how flesh is inhabited with meaning. Inhabiting the world involves self-knowledge, art and science, labours for justice, and healing, for a world in which there is no hunger and thirst for justice would be a world of flesh.[11]

The idea of the world becoming inhabited draws on the image Jesus used of an untenanted or uninhabited space into which flow the forces of destruction (Matthew 12.43–45). Jesus' healing Williams describes as restoring of relation and inclusion in the community. It is the bridging of a gulf between spirit and empty or alienated flesh. People who are healed or exorcized by Christ come to be places inhabited by love, by thanksgiving, by peace and by the sense of absolution. Acts of healing free people to express what they are made and called to be, which is members of a community that lives in gratitude and praise, members of a community in which flesh gives voice to spirit and, in so doing, creates further networks of healing, integrating relation (Mark 1.40—2.12).

So, just as the self becomes soul, so the flesh becomes body, a community, including the community of the body of Christ, the Church. Each person is formed by and forms the communities of which he or she is a part. Community allows for many styles of life, but people do not become a random collection of eccentrics in the monastic community, because it lays stress upon obedience and attending to others, and is a place where the two essentials of Christian life, love and humility, are lived out and so community can flourish. Christian commitment refuses any freezing of relationships, for penitence implies active change. Peace, health and reconciliation are all images, Williams writes, that Christians are perennially tempted to see in passive, naturalistic or static ways, and all of them can represent refusals of the world.

Being in love is one example of the way in which flesh is inhabited and how relationships bring this about. Being in love is the experience of two people in which each is accepted, given time and room, and treated not as an object of desire alone but as a focus for attention and fascination. Both partners in love long to find a way of expressing and discovering truth about themselves, because they have been given a kind of promise. The promise is a promise of someone being shown to themselves in ways that couldn't otherwise have been realized. We discover ourselves by a twofold process of listening to the other partner and searching for words to describe the reality of the self we cannot see but are now assured is there.[12]

Listening, attentiveness and allowing people the freedom to be themselves is what enables flesh to be inhabited. Attention and love go hand in hand in any community, though in contemporary society the skills of being present for and in another have been eroded and what remains is mistrust and violence. The Christian community, however, has the task of teaching us so to order our relations that human beings may see themselves as desired, as the occasion of joy.

## Healthy relationships

Relationships are not always healthy, however. Being in love intensifies our sense of self as well as confronting us with someone else, and the balance needs to be healthy. If it is towards egotism, there may come a point when we want to mould or control the interests of the other. If the balance is towards self-denial, we may no longer see ourselves as solid and complex. If our worth is wholly bound up with another person, we will be terrified of losing ourselves if we lose the other and so can efface our own agenda and allow ourselves to be invaded or exploited.

Christian witness may well involve resistance to forms of human community, including the family, for any human group whose policy or programme it is to pursue its interest at the direct cost of others has no claim on the Christian's loyalty in itself. Williams is clear that the Church does not either affirm or deny the family in the abstract but is authorized to ask of any human association whether it is making it more or less difficult for people to grow into a maturity in which they are free to give to one another and nourish one another: free enough to know they have the capacity to be involved in recreating persons. Where forms of human belonging are manifestly at odds with the kingdom resistance may be the most important Christian service, such as that of Dietrich Bonhoeffer in the Third Reich.

The forging of right relationships is important in the pastoral context. The qualities necessary in a pastor are self-awareness and mutuality. Pastors are to be humble rather than superior, and have an understanding of both the human condition and its potential in Christ. Superiority in the pastor damages both people in the pastoral relationship. No one is entitled to judge and thus assume they have arrived at a settled spiritual maturity that entitles them to prescribe confidently and at a distance for another. That leaves them without the therapy they need for their souls and cuts them off from God, as well as the one judging. Pastors need to have 'been there' and be self-aware. Priests need familiarity with the face of humanity, Williams writes, as well as fidelity in prayer, a habit of gratitude and a level of detachment, not from human suffering or human delight, but from dependence on human achievement. What plausibility is there in the words of someone who seems to see less in the world than others, whose understanding of the murkiness of human motivation and the frequency of human failure is smaller than that of the average believer? We cannot uncover the face of Christ in people unless we have had that real attention to human faces in all their diversity – but also the habit of familiarity with the face of Christ.[13]

## THE JOURNEY FROM ADVERSITY TO ALTRUISM: SPEECH AND SPACE

Williams attends to the dynamics of developing altruism and pastoral responsibility in his theology and does so using the metaphor of space. Speech, as we have seen, is a central metaphor for Williams in his exploration of the relationship of human creatures to God. God summons them into being and they are then formed in conversation with others. When it comes to the development of altruism, compassion and love, space is the central metaphor as Williams explores the Christian virtue of detachment and the need for breathing spaces and hesitation in order to respond to others and create the possibility of change.

### Detachment and breathing spaces

It may seem surprising that a theologian who emphasizes relationships so strongly would promote the monastic virtue of detachment. Williams does so however by seeing it not as a strategy of disengagement but the condition for serious involvement. Williams explores the ideal of detachment, not as loss, distance and isolation or a withdrawal from ordinary feeling or obligation, but as a kind of passion that liberates instead of enslaving.[14]

Detachment gives space and balance in relating to situations and to people. Detachment is neither being defended against the suffering of the world nor helplessly submerged in it. It is a kind of compassion that is not simply a visceral feeling of solidarity but an awareness of another's suffering as other. This means that not every tragedy becomes one's own personal tragedy so that the focus of concern remains essentially on oneself. Detachment does not mean avoiding feeling, but feeling fully in a way that is not merely trust and interest in one's own feelings. Without detachment people become tyrants or slaves. An inability to come to terms with mortality brings people to rule by force, overriding and negating others, or alternatively being crushed by this force from others. Detachment enables people to be fully aware and attentive to reality, aware of tensions and the collision of concerns. To be detached means to be open to the possibility of engagement and action which is not uncritical, fearful or tentative but conscious of the risks it takes. Detachment as a Christian ideal means trusting in God with a trust that does not seek control over the future. It means surrendering the struggle to master the world and a dispossession that involves being open to God.

The development of the virtue of detachment enables compassion and altruistic engagement with the world, a working for understanding, for justice and against violence. The process of such growth happens by attending to a breathing space or moment of hesitation. The empty space resources a person or community to be self-aware, to develop empathy and to choose to act so that things may be different.

A breathing space or an empty space where we live in the presence of the void is an image Williams uses in reflecting on responses to September 11, 2001 and its aftermath. He takes the image from the account of a woman accused of adultery where Jesus at first makes no reply but writes with his finger in the dust. His hesitation, Williams says, gives people time to see themselves differently because he refuses to make the sense they want him to. Such a holding of the moment for a little longer, Williams writes, can be long enough for some of our demons to walk away.[15] Such a breathing space is, of course, a desert place of its own: it enables movement through the desert metaphor I have used which begins in adversity and, moving through self-awareness, is expressed through altruism.

The emptiness of the breathing space resources us, Williams says, because there is some space between our feelings and choices which encourages the development of empathy. This gives us an ability to put our immediate feelings on hold, resist the longing to re-establish control, and consider our desires and responses.

Trauma can offer a breathing space that shows us a door into the suffering of countless other innocents, often a suffering that is more or less routine for them in their less regularly protected environments. A breathing space enables the possibility of change by providing an opportunity to respond and by giving room to the perspective of others, rather than clinging harder to our threatened identity or fear that we are powerless. Such a response requires courage and imagination not to be passive and not to be the victim, but equally not to avoid passivity by simply reproducing what's been done to you.

Breathing spaces present the possibility of choice. God is encountered as a human person creates his or her life in choosing for or against self-gratifying instinct, for or against power and violence, for or against communion, for or against obedience to the creator. The significant elements of a human life, Williams says, are in these moments of precariousness, of the sense of the possibility of freedom. This space for breathing is analogous to the desert experience where direction and priorities can be set in a landscape that is differentiated from any other and provides the place to go within the self and emerge changed.

## The descent and the return

The virtue of detachment popularized by Williams's description of breathing spaces describes the perspective of a mature Christian who has experienced adversity, been strengthened by it and is able to feel and to act altruistically. Such acts of compassion bring healing and lead to pastoral responsibility. Williams describes the heart of saintliness as expressed in people returning to the lost, the excluded, the failed or destroyed after the pattern of Jesus, who having experienced suffering can claim authority only by returning to help those who continue to suffer. Williams points to the great theological myth of the descent into hell, where God's presence in the world in Jesus is seen as his journey into the furthest deserts of despair and alienation. He shows his inexhaustible mercy for all by identifying even with the lost. In some elusive and paradoxical way, this myth speaks of one human destiny, realized in and through Jesus. He comes to his new and risen life, his universal kingship, by searching out all the forgotten and failed members of his family. Only in this way can he claim authority in heaven and on earth.

## Summary

Rowan Williams presents a contemporary Christian theology resonant with the findings of resilience literature and drawing on the biblical and theological tradition. His understanding is of the self formed in relationship to other people, with struggle and risk leading to honesty about the human condition as dependent and limited by space and time, but free, created by a God who does not need us to forge identity, but creates as pure gift and as love. Williams uses and interprets the traditional concepts of Christian teaching such as dependence, obedience, humility, detachment, self-denial and dying to self. Aware of their misuse, Williams explores them in such a way that openness to relationships and affirmation of the body are not undermined. His vision of the mature Christian life means that the pastor will be continually open to the growth that draws him or her to the cross and resurrection by being shaped and shaping others, practising contemplation and developing a detachment that enables compassion and is open to hurt, pain and risk as well as political action. Williams's presentation of the dynamics of strengthening through adversity provides the understanding required for resilient believing.

# CHAPTER SIX

# From wounded healer to resilient pastor

## FEELING THE PAIN AS A PASTOR

I have become familiar with what happens to me when I receive a phone call to tell me that someone for whom I have pastoral responsibility is now at the point of death, or has been diagnosed with a terminal illness, or has been bereaved. When I have put the phone down I breathe in slowly and go through the first cycle of despair, resistance and commitment. My first instincts are of despair and resistance. Despair at another human tragedy, the unfairness, the waste or pain for whoever is involved, and then the resistance in me, in the face of my role, of meeting need, of providing whatever is required of me. My instinct is to run away, or hide – somehow to deny or avoid having anything to do with whatever horror I have just been told about. The resistance comes from my reluctance to witness more anguish, to again find that such anguish echoes my own in the form of memories of the past or fears for the future. Resistance comes too from the expectations of myself and others that I can somehow help, bring comfort or perform a miracle. In a matter of seconds, my out-breaths can become those of commitment to other human beings in their time of need, commitment to God to discover where he may be found, and commitment to myself to care for myself in order to be of help in the present and sane in the future. Putting the phone down engenders the first of many cycles. To go through them enables me to form and grow as a resilient pastor.

The metaphor of the desert has given us three stages to journey through in order to be strengthened in adversity. Embracing the desert and encountering the self are the first two stages, which I have just described in my experience of despair and resistance on receiving a pastoral call. In the third stage, as studies in resilience reveal, resilient people find healing for themselves as they work for healing others by altruistic activity or pastoral responsibility. It is hard to read much about pastoral care without coming across the model of the wounded healer. The myths and model of the wounded healer explore the relationship between a pastor's personal history of adversity and pastoral ministry, and thus the dynamics of healing in a pastoral relationship. Many of us have come across pastors whose experience of life and ministry has involved suffering and whose pain is palpable through their sympathy and care. How might they, and any pastor, journey in a way that brings healing, maturity, growth and strengthening?

This chapter explores the ways in which the myths and model of the wounded healer help pastors to form and grow so that they are strengthened in the exercise of their pastoral ministry. Exploring the dynamics of the wounded healer builds on what we have seen so far in the narratives of Hagar and Moses: their pastoral responsibility was born out of adversity and, in Moses' case, having 'been there' gave him the credentials to lead the people. The themes within the myths and model of the wounded healer echo the qualities of the monastic elders we have looked at, the abbas or ammas, described as healers rather than teachers for whom humility and discernment are key qualities. That relationship is characterized by obedience, humility and trust. Williams recognizes, within those virtues, the importance of autonomy and response in relating, as well as the need to deepen pain after the pattern of Christ, be continually open to growth, and recognize that superiority enslaves both the pastor and those for whom he or she cares.

## THE WOUNDED HEALER: A MODEL FOR THE PASTOR

The wounded healer as a pastoral care model of ministry – though not the myth itself – has been made popular for Christians by

Henri Nouwen. The model is commonly used in the teaching of pastoral care to affirm that wounds, or experiences of adversity, in the life of the pastor need to be acknowledged and can be a resource for healing others and for the pastor. As a metaphor of ministry and priesthood which emphasizes the idea of the wounded healer who is working towards becoming more whole, it is linked to similar metaphors of ministry such as 'wounded companion', 'pain bearer' and 'wilderness person'.[1]

The model of the wounded healer, however, has weaknesses of which I want pastors to be aware. Rarely are the Greek myths of the wounded healer ever explored when pastors consider the model. In this chapter, I will explore the myth of Chiron and the use of the wounded healer in teaching pastors. I will discuss the ways in which the model can help pastors understand the dynamics of healing by drawing on ministry with the dying and the insights of psychotherapy. My hope is to strengthen the model of the wounded healer by incorporating the contribution of resilience literature and desert experience, and propose the model of the Resilient Pastor, a reinterpretation of the wounded healer appropriate for our time.

## CHIRON THE CENTAUR: WOUNDED AND RESILIENT

The origins of the wounded-healer myths are ancient, expressed in the Greek myths that depict Asclepius and Chiron as wounded healers. Asclepius was the son of the sun god, Apollo, and the human woman Coronis. He was wounded before his birth because Apollo had instigated the shooting of Coronis while she was pregnant because she had been unfaithful. While Coronis was on the funeral pyre Apollo tore his son from her womb and gave him to Chiron to raise and mentor. He became a healer.

The myth of Chiron explores the dynamics of strengthening and healing through adversity. Chiron was born a centaur, with a human head and torso and the body of a horse, because he was conceived when his father, one of the gods, disguised in the form of a horse, raped a mortal nymph. He was consequently immortal. Having been abandoned and rejected at birth, he was adopted by the sun god Apollo, who reared him and taught him all he knew.

Chiron became a wise and respected teacher, renowned for his shrewd intelligence and many skills. He was mentor to some of Greece's greatest heroes, including Hercules. Chiron was civilized and cultured, but centaurs were renowned for their tendency to become violent after drinking wine. One day, at a wedding banquet, fighting broke out between an unruly group of drunk centaurs and the rest of the guests. Hercules, who was among the guests, fired a poisoned arrow at the centaurs to stop the rioting, but Chiron happened to be standing in their midst and the arrow struck him in the knee. As Chiron was immortal, a poisoned arrow could not kill him but instead it inflicted an agonizing and unhealable wound. For the first half of Chiron's life his experience was of success and acclaim among the kings and heroes of Greece. In the second part he fled to the mountains to tend his wound and began a desperate search for release from his suffering. While he could not find his own cure, he became wise in the use of all forms of healing herbs and showed compassion to the suffering of others. The blind, the lame and those in pain came to him and he welcomed them and brought them comfort. They called him the wounded healer for he could not heal himself. One day Hercules brought news that if Chiron were willing to sacrifice his immortality on behalf of Prometheus, who was being punished for mocking the gods, he could be freed of his suffering. Chiron agreed to this, died and descended to the underworld. For nine days and nine nights he remained in the darkness of death. Then Zeus, recognizing the generosity of the sacrifice, took pity on Chiron and restored his immortality, raising him to the heavens as a constellation of stars.

These myths resonate with everything that has come before in this book about the ways in which people are strengthened through adversity. The experience of adversity, combined with an inner life, described in the myths as the journey within, strengthens people in such a way that they are drawn to helping others. We see this in the narratives of Hagar and Moses. In the Chiron myth we see healing bound up with relationships with others: it is at the invitation of another, and for the sake of others, that Chiron makes the decision to offer himself as a sacrifice that brings about healing for himself and other people. The desert Christians are revered as healers rather than teachers, and we see that Chiron began as a mentor and teacher and became a wise healer. Complete healing for Chiron comes with the decision to let go, but, as in Cassian's theology, this is beyond altruism and beyond the confines of this life. Themes of struggle, self and relationships are prominent. In the journey from adversity to altruism seen in the myths the emphasis is on healing and involves further adversity, a willingness to undergo further pain or self-sacrifice.

## THE PASTOR AS WOUNDED HEALER

Henri Nouwen is almost synonymous with the phrase 'wounded healer' in Christian circles. He wrote his book *The Wounded Healer* for those ministering in a contemporary society, in a dislocated world with a rootless generation. Nouwen argues that the minister must be the articulator of the inner events of his or her own life, must exhibit a compassion that avoids the distance of pity and the exclusivity of sympathy, and must be contemplative – to break the vicious cycle of immediate needs asking for immediate satisfaction. Christian leadership, he writes, must exhibit not only faith and hope, but personal concern: 'Who can take away suffering without entering it? The great illusion of leadership is to think that man can be led out of the desert by someone who has never been there.'[2]

It is in the last chapter, entitled 'Ministry by a lonely minister', that Nouwen explores the image of the wounded healer. He drew his inspiration from the image in a rabbinical story of a man at the city gates who, rather than unbinding all his wounds at the same time like the others sitting begging at the gate, unbound only one at a time and then bound it up again, saying to himself, 'Perhaps I shall be needed; if so, I must always be ready so as not to delay for a moment.' What Nouwen drew from the story was the faithful tending of one's own woundedness, which he described as the wounded minister, and the willingness to move to the aid of other people and make the fruits of woundedness available to others, which he described as the healing minister. The wounds that Nouwen identifies are those of personal loneliness, which he describes as a gift and sweet pain which must be guarded as a source for human understanding, and professional loneliness. The latter results from the minister's desire to provide meaning that is not always welcomed in churches, which Nouwen describes as 'little more than parlours for those who feel comfortable with the old life'.

Nouwen holds that all human beings are wounded to a greater or lesser extent. The process of facilitating the healing of another is thus made possible because all pastors have been there, to some extent have suffered, and can heal others because they have come through, developed empathy and formed the ability to heal by the way in which they relate to others. The minister heals by seeing his or her own pain and suffering as rising from the depth of the human condition which all people share. By not running away from the pains of others, but touching them with compassion and healing, new strength is brought so that 'the paradox indeed is [that] the beginning of healing is in the solidarity with the pain'.

Healing takes place through hospitality for Nouwen. This is because the host feels at home in his house and so is able to create a free and fearless place for the unexpected visitor, paying attention to the guest, and practising meditation and contemplation. Nouwen uses the image of desert hospitality, comparing pastors to Semitic nomads who live in a desert with many lonely travellers who are looking for a moment of peace, a fresh drink and a sign of encouragement so that they can continue their mysterious search for freedom. The healer creates a kind of hospitality that requires an empty space where the guest can find his or her own soul, for wholeness cannot be given from one to another – rather, the loneliness can be understood, faced and accepted as part of the human condition.

Nouwen's use of 'wounded healer' reveals the aspects of self-awareness and attention to growth that are necessary for resilience and were encouraged by the desert Christians; his own term is 'faithful tending', which leads to compassion. The quality of the pastoral relationship that he describes as hospitality draws a detachment that creates space and yet is fully involved, as the desert tradition and Williams outline. Adversity and pain, part of human life and pastoral ministry, are what bring empathy. What is starkly different in Nouwen's account of the pastor as a wounded healer is the choice the pastor has, unlike Chiron or

those in adversity. In the myth of Chiron and in the lives of the
resilient the struggle is to survive. There is very little choice about
acknowledging wounds and seeking health because not to do so
has such serious and immediate consequences. Nouwen is encouraging pastors to recognize that their own sense of woundedness,
professional and personal, is common to all humanity and can
be a resource in their pastoral ministry. Many Christians will be
unwilling to acknowledge, much less look again at, painful times
in their past that they had hoped to have left behind. Nouwen
can only encourage pastors to see their wounds in this way – it is
adversity itself that provides the need to do so. Of course, during
a pastor's ministry he or she will, in the ordinary way of life, meet
adversity, and so opportunity presents itself to build resilience
that has fruits for ministry.

Other writers on pastoral theology have also taken up the
wounded-healer model to explore the role of the pastor. Alastair
Campbell uses three images of caring in his search to rediscover a
Christian understanding of pastoral care based on personal integrity, without which, he says, ecclesiastical role or counselling tech-
niques are of no use. His images are that of the shepherd, wise
folly and the wounded healer. Campbell, like Nouwen, emphasizes
the need for self-awareness in the pastor. For Campbell the person
of integrity is 'first and foremost a critic of self, of tendencies to
self deception and escape from reality, of desire for a false inner
security in place of the confrontation with truth which integrity
demands. Pastoral care is grounded in mutuality, not expertise, so
that in finding some courage, hope and transcendence in the midst
of life a pastor can help another find that same wholeness.' The
wounded healer heals, he says, 'because he or she is able to convey,
as much by presence as by the words used, both an awareness and
a transcendence of loss'. Loss he describes, of all human experiences, as the 'most pervasive and potentially the most crippling'.
Wounded healers heal because they, 'to some degree at least, have
entered the depths of their own experiences of loss and in those
depths found hope again'.[3]

Pastoral care, for Campbell, is derived from vulnerability, which
he explores by using the language of wounds. Responding to
the wounds, the vulnerability of others forms community and a

channel of communication from one isolated individual to another, with blood becoming the seal of reconciliation. Without drawing on the Greek myths, Campbell uses the woundedness of Jesus to undergird the wounded-healer model. He describes the wounded healer as an image of care central to the Christian understanding of the significance of Jesus' death. Jesus' wounds are 'the expressions of his openness to our suffering', and such 'wounded love has a healing power because it is enfleshed love, entering into human weakness, feeling our pain standing beside us in our dereliction'. Campbell points to Christ's humility (Philippians 2.8), the image of the Suffering Servant (Isaiah 53.5) and the ransom of the Son of Man (Matthew 20.28) as ways of healing, because it is in this utter weakness that the power of God is found, in the depths of human degradation and cruelty, in deepest darkness that we find the flame of love, in the intertwining of suffering and strength.[4]

Pastoral theologians describe the experience of adversity and coming through it as key to helping others. They emphasize the motif of the wounded healer to encourage pastors to recognize their own life story and the way in which it impacts on their ministry – particularly the experience of suffering. It is this experience, drawn upon, they recognize, that develops empathy and the ability to facilitate healing. It echoes the first stage of the desert metaphor necessary to begin a process of resilience – embracing the desert.

My observation of the emphasis on the wounded-healer motif is that it emphasizes woundedness rather than healing. Such emphasis is placed on enabling students and pastors to acknowledge and explore their wounds, and warning how not to do so can bring damage to others, that much less attention is given to how this can be part of the process of healing in pastoral ministry. Campbell and Nouwen both recognize the danger. Once pastors are self-aware enough to recognize their own woundedness they need to attend to their wounds so that they may be of service to others, otherwise they cause damage. Campbell reminds us that wounds do not restore health. They lead to healing 'only when they have been uncovered and dealt with; otherwise they are festering sores which destroy our health and the health of those with whom we deal'. Nouwen warns of a spiritual exhibitionism where the minister tells others that he or she has the same problems: this is of no help, since open wounds stink rather than heal. Once pastors have recognized the adversity of their personal history they may not get any further. They see the desert but do not embrace it as the beginning of a process of resilience.

Another danger for pastors – related to the emphasis on woundedness – is colluding with others who will not recognize the adversity, or, to put it another way, will not embrace the desert. Preachers, teachers and pastors who emphasize the peace of Christ as a quiet and passive quality, and do not declare struggle as a healthy and necessary response to difficulty which helps you realize what matters to you and provides the energy to carry it out, collude with those still in denial masked as faith. Of course, advice to trust God can close down difficult conversations which a pastor might wish to avoid because it is hard to witness fear and pain and know one does not have the answers. A naive religious faith can be used as a defence against the harsh realities of life. The pretence at invulnerability in churches and the denial of the raw vulnerabilities of life, Campbell declares, drain the churches of compassion and make them able to tolerate only those who can conceal their ill health. Campbell and Nouwen recognize that ministry is a very confronting service because, as Nouwen puts it, 'it does not allow people to live with the illusions of immortality and wholeness, but reminds others that they are mortal and broken but also that with the recognition of this condition, liberation starts'. The pastor helps others by a steadfast refusal to collude in their wish to avoid the reality of loss and the terror this can bring, since 'pastoral care does not remove pain: it deepens it . . . to a level where it can be shared'. Such a refusal to collude can be conveyed in preaching and teaching as well as in one-to-one conversations which allow people to feel safe enough to let down their defences and face the truth about their situation.

So pastors can pretend they have never suffered personally and collude with Christian communities who would also prefer to pretend they are invulnerable. A pastor can also recognize and exhibit woundedness, causing damage in pastoral relationships. The experience of woundedness, once acknowledged, can be overwhelming – as my own experience and so my exploration of how pastors can be strengthened recognizes. To compare the cost of pastoral care for the pastor, as Campbell does, to the experience of Jesus, whose physical wounds were from torture and psychological wounds from personal betrayal that led to execution, is very stark. This points to something of the strength of the impact that pastors can experience in caring for those in adversity.

My sense is that the issue of woundedness in the personal history of a pastor and its relationship to pastoral ministry is opened up by pastoral theologians as they use the model of the wounded healer to teach new pastors to acknowledge their own sufferings. It is not, however, fully explored and thus balanced with the healing aspect of the wounded-healer motif. In the pastoral model, as opposed to the Greek myth, we do not find people flocking to the pastor as they did to Asclepius and Chiron, and coming away healed. The model does not provide a strong sense of healer, or an understanding of the dynamics of healing or strengthening in adversity. The model also tends towards putting the pastor in a superior position as wounded healer, who 'gains power' by acknowledging weakness, as Campbell puts it. There is little sense or exploration of mutuality in relating, or of how pain is shared so that love can enter.

## THE WOUNDED-HEALER RELATIONSHIP AND THE DYING

Michael Kearney, a consultant in palliative medicine, explored the nature of soul pain and healing in those close to death. His theory and technique of inner care uses image work and draws on the myth of the wounded healer in a way that is independent of, but not antagonistic to, religious doctrine. Kearney uses the myth of Chiron, which he sees as an ancient reworking of shamanic initiation of the Palaeolithic era at the dawning of human consciousness. He uses the myth to describe the journey that someone in adversity, indeed dying, takes. This involves struggling and then trusting a process which is in fact strengthening.

Multidisciplinary work in palliative care has taken up the concept of resilience, affirming the importance of self-esteem, relationships and struggle, and encompassing spiritual care, work with families and carers, rehabilitation and bereavement. The process of strengthening in facing a terminal illness is intimately related to the sense of self and helped by relationships with other human beings. One such relationship can be with a wounded healer. In his use of the Chiron myth, Kearney explores the dynamics of the doctor or healer's relationship with the patient. He recognizes the importance of the healer's wounds and, as we shall see, explores how they bring about healing. Kearney's contribution affirms the themes of struggle, self and relationships as key components in the journey from adversity to altruism and beyond, to a healing through death. He affirms the importance of the personal history of the pastor and the need to be steadfast in the face of pain, as a witness to the pain of others and one's own pain. In a way that echoes the relationship of the desert elder, humility and mutuality are significant for a healing relationship, as is the development of trust that enables someone to embark on a painful journey within.

Kearney describes Western medicine as comparable to the time in Chiron's life where he struggled to find a cure for his mortal wound and in doing so healed many others. This heroic stance or struggle underpins the medical model of healing with diagnosis, treatment and cure. This works well until one is faced with insoluble problems where simply trying harder to find a cure will not work and an emotional pain is engendered, characterized by feelings of frustration, powerlessness and fear of what the future might hold. Kearney uses the Chiron myth to chart the process of healing in five parts: the wounding, the struggle, the choice, the descent and the return.

When Chiron accepts the invitation to free Prometheus by descending to the underworld there is a paradigm shift from the heroic stance to the way of descent, and it is this which is the gateway to healing. Both the heroic stance of struggle and the way of descent are essential in the process of dying, with struggle dominating the earliest stages where the wound may not be mortal and cure may be found. The struggle also helps to create the emotional conditions that facilitate the shift, so that all know the struggle has achieved everything it can and that to continue to struggle is damaging, futile and adding to pain and suffering. Struggle brings people struggling more fully into themselves and slows them down so that they become acquainted with suffering and weary of it, and so more ready to descend. The adversity can open up access to some hitherto hidden inner resources and trigger a growth process.[5]

Enabling this shift to happen is the focus of healing for Kearney. Struggle prepares for this descent into the depths of oneself. Chiron's choice to surrender immortality is the choice of the patient and the carer to let go of the illusion of omnipotence. They cannot cure the wound by continuing to struggle, but the struggle to cure by those who care can forge trust and enable the shift to take place, not because of some special intervention but spontaneously. When a dying person enters the descent into depth he or she is experienced in a very different way despite external circumstances not having changed. Kearney describes a patient becoming a wounded healer so that instead of 'feeling impotent, and failure, guilty, panicky and drained, I now came away feeling enriched as though I was learning something very important from him'. This is an indication of the fifth stage of return.

Struggle is affirmed in this reading of the Chiron myth as enabling cure and later the conditions from which trust and journey within the depths of the self take place. The pastor can experience both the wounds and the healing in the pastoral relationship. A good pastor is one who has learnt to use his or her own feelings diagnostically. When feeling panic, a pastor has to discern, and with self-awareness can discern, whose panic it is – her own or the person she is with. Pastors can feel someone else's pain and can also facilitate and experience healing. Carers, doctors and pastors can experience both the soul pain of the wounded person and the return, where the shift and descent has taken place. Kearney describes the total pain of someone facing death as having social, emotional and spiritual, as well as physical, components. Soul, for Kearney, is associated with depth, death and the imagination, and soul pain is a symptom of the ego's total identification with the surface mind and its resistance to descent into depth. Soul pain can be recognized by the feelings and behaviour patterns it awakens in carers. Confronted by an insoluble problem, carers find that the 'pain which we cannot control triggers our own ego survival reactions' so that 'we do, we do even and when we do not succeed, we go on doing.' In pastoral ministry there is often talk about the importance of 'being' rather than 'doing.' The solution to soul pain is to point inwards and downwards to the roots of our humanity because reconnection with depth is required. For many people, physical, emotional and social care are enough for them to commit themselves to their inner descent. For others specific intervention such as image work, dream, art, music, reminiscence or biography therapy, body work, including massage, and certain forms of meditation are helpful.

Healing comes about within the relating and requires mutuality and humility reminiscent both of the relationship with the desert elder and the therapeutic relationships described by Williams. Kearney describes the relationship of patient and client shifting to a wounded-healer relationship as they become present to each other as human beings standing on the edge of the known and searching together for a path forward. Here, who is wounded and who is healer is much less clear. Indeed, both in searching for healing and in reaching out to another we become wounded healers to ourselves as well as to others. Recognizing this dynamic is vital, for unless we do we will either mistakenly continue to believe that we as carers always have the answers to other people's problems, or as patients continue searching in never-ending circles for that someone or something 'out there' who will at last take all our pain away. The tragedy in this is that we may never pause long enough to realize that the way to the healing we desire is, in fact, seeking us out, and always as close to us as we are to ourselves. The moment we wait for, which some call grace, is not so much a matter of finding the deep centre as being found by it, says Kearney.

Kearney's exploration of the Chiron myth makes a significant contribution to furthering the Christian reading of the myths and model of the wounded healer. He does so specifically in relationship to dying, of course, which is a significant component of pastoral work and takes the pastor beyond the scope of resilience literature. He addresses the healing aspect of the wounded healer by emphasizing the mutuality of the wounded-healer relationship. The pastor experiences the pain of the person in adversity, and, if self-aware, can use this as a trigger to facilitate healing in the other and in doing so also experience healing. This description takes us further than that of the pastoral care model. Both the pastoral care model and the palliative care model point to the need for steadfastness in the face of the lure to provide easy answers for people. Kearney acknowledges the pull to *do*, rather than sit with another in the face of death, but it is the refusal to *do* that shows the direction needed for healing. Nouwen and Campbell describe the need for an inward and downward shift by speaking of contemplation, meditation and integrity. Kearney goes further in identifying that when this shift to descend takes place, in pastor as well as patient, it travels deeper than vulnerability and acknowledgement of weakness, to a depth where healing and grace seek us out for healing. This takes place when both pastor and patient are motivated to seek healing for themselves and able to reach out in compassion. Choice is important in Kearney's process of healing. Letting go into the depths requires trust in the self and in others which is often facilitated by someone who has shared the struggle to find a cure. The journey cannot be brought about by a passive or blind obedience, but can be enabled by a relationship of mutuality and trust.

Kearney's description of healing reveals where a development of Campbell's use of the death and woundedness of Christ as wounded healer might go. Campbell addresses the Wounding, the Struggle and the Choice of Kearney's five parts of the process of healing, through the narratives of Gethsemane and the crucifixion. Descent and Return might be explored with reference to Christ's descent into hell and God's initiative in raising him to new life, as indeed Williams does. Healing, restoration and connection are what come about through Christ's descent, resurrection and return.

## THE DANGERS OF BEING A WOUNDED HEALER: WARNINGS FROM JUNGIAN PSYCHOLOGY

In Jungian psychology the wounded healer is recognized as an archetype, an image or predisposition to behave and conceptualize the world in certain ways, partly inherited and partly arising from the circumstances of our upbringing. Carl Jung used the archetype of the wounded healer, deriving it from the ancient Greek

legend of Asclepius, to explore dimensions of counter-transference, the impact on the therapist of unconscious processes in a
therapeutic relationship. Here we need to recognize the dynamics
of the wounded-healer relationship detailed by Jung, as well as
its dangers. In psychological literature, following Jung, it is the
dangers inherent in the wounded healer that are emphasized, so
that the model is treated with suspicion, if not rejected.

Significant dynamics of relating, both in general and particularly in therapeutic relationships, are described in the literature
of psychotherapy and counselling using the concepts of transference and counter-transference. Transference is an unconscious
phenomenon where the client projects attitudes, feelings and
desires, originally linked with early significant persons, on to the
therapist who represents these figures in the client's current life.
One can use the term more generally to label any feelings that the
client expresses towards the therapist, a pastor or anyone else.
Clergy are one group particularly prone to having people trans-
fer the dynamics of previous relationships on to them, because
people sense and respond to something in themselves that triggers a past relationship, often with an authority figure such as a
teacher or parent. Therapists and others involved in the helping
professions have transference reactions in response. If a member
of a congregation is relating in a way that seems odd to you it may
be that they are transferring feelings they had for the stern father
of an ex-girlfriend on to you and expecting you to react to them as
that person did. You may feel lured into playing the role. Counter-
transference is a therapist's or pastor's counter-reaction to transference. It is what gets stimulated in the therapist in response to
what the client is experiencing and can be described as intuition
about what the client is feeling. It is the therapist's or pastor's
personal experiences, in particular, that are activated, especially
if they are similar, and they can range from curiosity to being overwhelmed. When pastors experience personal pain as they exercise their pastoral ministry, as in the way that Kearney describes
feeling the soul pain of a dying person, the pain is described in
psychological terms as counter-transference. The counter-transference dynamic needs to be understood by the pastor in order that
growth and healing – indeed strengthening – can come about in

the relationship. Here the wounded healer is a relationship rather than a person, undermining an emphasis on the pastor as superior and in control and yet pointing to why pastors might feel the need to be so.

Jung was one of the first psychoanalysts to stress the therapeutic potential of counter-transference, observing that 'only the wounded doctor can heal, whether that doctor be a physician or a priest'. Jung described the way in which a therapist's wounds may be activated in certain situations, especially if the patient's wounds are similar to those of the therapist. Jung felt that this type of depth psychology can be potentially dangerous, because the analyst is vulnerable to having his or her wounds reopened. The two dangers for the wounded healer to watch out for are 'inflation and death', that is, a defended superiority or being overwhelmed by pain. The dangers can be avoided by realizing that the personal involvement and healing processes are archetypically based. Realizing this can help deflate the over-zealous or overwhelmed analyst. The extremely popular American television series *House*, with the British actor Hugh Laurie, portrays a brilliant diagnostician, Gregory House, who can be described as a wounded healer, but is perhaps better described as an unhealed wounder. House exemplifies the inflationary danger of a wounded healer, which in fact prevents healing and relating well. Physically wounded in the leg, House cures others by his uncanny perception and brilliant mind. He also uses these skills to play his colleagues off against one another. His arrogance prevents him from experiencing any healing or strengthening personally. Indeed, he avoids the wounded-healer relationship by rarely actually meeting the patient. House typifies the dangers of being a wounded healer to the doctor or pastor, as well as those around them.

Within the 'school of the wounded healer' – that is, those who draw on the archetype in the discussion of counter-transference from a Jungian perspective – it is humility and mutuality in the analyst that counteract the dangers of an inflated ego or being overwhelmed by pain. People in the helping professions do have a particular fascination with this 'bipolar archetype', which is dangerous if the sickness side of it is left entirely with the patient. To avoid this analysts must be aware of their own shadow side, and acknowledging their own woundedness realize like the Greek physician that only the divine healer can help, and that they can be part of facilitating the process. The development of the inner healer in the patient comes by the activation of woundedness in the analyst, and the analyst must show the way by experiencing the archetype and its ramifications personally.

A Jungian understanding of counter-transference affirms the experience of costliness to the pastor described in pastoral care literature. Experienced pastors know that there are some pastoral situations that will be difficult for them personally because they have experienced a similar situation, such as the death of a child or a particular type of illness. It may be that when it comes to it, and perhaps because they have given space to their own feelings and memories, it doesn't feel as bad as was feared. Some situations really get to a pastor and it is not immediately, or indeed ever, obvious as to why. This kind of pain or cost is beyond the normal level experienced by the pastor when involved in sad and tragic events. It is beyond the empathy caused by adversity in general. The painful feelings are described as counter-transference wounds. There seems to be a fundamental difference in degree and quality in empathy, and in counter-transference wounds which are triggered where the pain of the patient or client is similar in some way to the history of the doctor, analyst or pastor. This pain however can provide the basis for empathy. It could cause the pastor to 'run away' and this will mean seeking a defence against the pain. The Jungian wounded-healer archetype is understood to work in relationships because the pastor conveys mutuality and humility. Running away means hiding behind a role – and one with power, so that humility and mutuality are undermined, if not negated. For the pastor to facilitate healing for others, he or she must lead the way, having been there. This echoes Williams's description of what is good for one being good for all – for healing comes either for both in the pastoral relationship or for neither party.

## CLERGY AS WOUNDED HEALERS

It is the dangers of the wounded-healer relationship that are prevalent in the literature of counselling and psychotherapy, echoing Jung's warnings, and describing unhealed wounders. The concept of the wounded healer, with rare exceptions, is defined in pejorative terms. This is because studies designed to explore the motivation of psychotherapists, in particular, have concluded that many have entered the field to heal their own wounds and have often been ineffective or even harmful in their interactions with their patients. Numerous studies have explored the fact that practitioners in the helping professions report a much higher incidence of troubled backgrounds than other people, concluding that 'the helping professions, notably psychotherapy and the ministry, appear to attract more than their fair share of the emotionally unstable'.[6] To work in the helping professions and yet remain unhealed creates damaging relationships. To use others as objects for one's own needs is unethical and destructive. Resilient people, as we have seen, report healing through helping others, but that has not been their conscious motivation for altruistic activity, though they are motivated towards taking responsibility for their personal growth.

It is possible to use pastoral ministry, just like other caring work, as a means of avoiding the need to deal with problems and gaining authority and power to compensate for weakness and vulnerability. Where this happens the professional can become divorced from the emotions that have brought pain, and become cold. Thomas Maeder identifies the clergy as providing conspicuous and instructive examples of those who encapsulate their wounds in this way: they develop a martyr complex where they believe that their self-denial serves a greater good, whereas in fact it is a self-directed keeping of the status quo where the wound does not cause pain, and is not susceptible to healing. Features of dysfunction he identifies include problems involving interpersonal relationships and questions of self-esteem. Giving too much, but not knowing how to take, leads finally to running out of spiritual and nervous energy so that what remains is underlying resentment. Pastoral encounters offer opportunities for living vicariously in the asymmetrical intimacy desired by those unwilling to take the painful risks incurred in normal human relationships.[7] Such a description of Christian pastors reveals that a lack of willingness to struggle, to grow, or to embrace the desert plays itself out in the sense of self and relationships of the pastor, who is not then able to find strength emerging from the experience of adversity in the past. It points to evidence of acedia among the clergy, the vice described by Cassian – the lack of self-care which causes either sleep at noon or an addiction to pastoral visiting that avoids encounter with the self or God. It is the vice of pastors, who need instead to recognize and pursue resilience as a virtue.

## THE RESILIENT PASTOR

The pastoral care model of the wounded healer is unbalanced in emphasizing woundedness to the detriment of healing and the person of the pastor to the detriment of the wounded-healer relationship. The model seeks to explore the connection between the woundedness of the pastor and the way in which this can serve the development of empathy, good pastoral care and healing, but it does not go far enough. The insights that Kearney brings from palliative care, and those of Jungian psychology, provide an understanding of the nature of the pastoral relationship that addresses these imbalances. They provide insights into motivation for pastoral ministry, the dynamics of healing through helping, the experience of being overwhelmed by pain that pastors can feel, and the importance of mutuality and humility for healing to occur. Thus much light is thrown on the question of how pastors can be strengthened as they exercise a ministry of pastoral care.

A model of pastoral care using the resilient pastor, however, can offer pastoral theology a model that not only builds positively on the wounded-healer model used in teaching pastoral care, but draws on the insights of resilience literature and the desert experience, providing pastors with a renewed understanding of the dynamics of healing in the pastoral relationship.

Although there are studies that have focused on the negative aspects of wounded healers, resilience literature abounds with studies of those who have come through their experience of early wounds and hurts and made them meaningful and the source for altruistic activity. Mary Bryant found in her research that resilient psychotherapists reported that it is not woundedness, but the denial of woundedness, that leads to impairment of a therapeutic or pastoral relationship. A wounded healer is not necessarily an impaired practitioner, but adequate self-assessment, boundary keeping and limit setting are vital, along with care and education, otherwise it is a short distance to becoming an impaired pastor or practitioner. The psychotherapists in her study described the wound as a gift, a gift of understanding and connection which enables the healing of others.

**Summary**

Resilience literature contributes to a reinterpretation of the pastoral care model of the wounded healer as resilient pastor by bringing to the fore the themes of struggle, self and relationships. The struggle to be self-aware, to continue to grow and to withstand emotional pain are essential for the pastor. Self-awareness enables a pastor to discern soul pain and facilitate healing. Self-discipline is required to maintain appropriate boundaries and develop an inner life which recognizes that there is a divine healer at work. The pastoral relationship of mutuality strengthens both of those involved.

The metaphor of the desert, enriched by the biblical and early Christian traditions of desert experience, reminds resilient pastors of their own need to embrace the desert. Such embracing of the desert brings an encounter with the self and with God. A pastoral ministry of serving others reflects the desert experience, where pastoral responsibility and leadership emerge because others recognize the credentials of someone who has suffered and come through with hope and compassion. The practices and wisdom of the desert Christians highlight the importance of humility, discernment and trust confirmed by the psychological understanding of the wounded-healer relationship. Whereas in the Greek myth of Chiron people flock to be healed, and in the archetype of the wounded-healer relationship healing takes place, the wounded-healer motif in Christian ministry can, in the model of the resilient pastor, find completion in a strengthening and healing by God for this life and beyond, for the pastor and those who are cared for.

# CHAPTER SEVEN

# A pastoral theology of resilience

---

## A PASTORAL THEOLOGY OF RESILIENCE

This book opened with my experience of formation as a pastor, beginning as I observed the dynamics of strengthening during my mother's illness when I was a child, through exercising a ministry of pastoral care as a priest, to having responsibility for the education and supervision of new pastors. My questions – how Christians, but particularly pastors, can help people going through adversity to be strengthened, and how pastors can be strengthened as they exercise a ministry of pastoral care – arose from these experiences.

I have taken the approach of critical conversation, choosing partners to listen to in order to draw on the richest possible resources and insights. The conversation began with studies in resilience and the biblical and Christian tradition of the desert. These conversations revealed themes and questions that led to a second stage of engagement – with the theology of Rowan Williams and with the way in which the myth of the wounded healer is used in secular pastoral practice and therapy as well as Christian pastoral care.

A pastoral theology of resilience has emerged: an integrated theological foundation that outlines the process and dynamics of strengthening in adversity and thus provides pastors and others with story and metaphor from the Christian tradition informed by psychosocial science to enable good practice in pastoral care.

## HELPING PEOPLE EXPERIENCING ADVERSITY TO BE STRENGTHENED: A THEOLOGICAL FOUNDATION

In resilience literature the themes identified as key to strengthening in adversity have been the importance of struggle in growth; an open, resourced and disciplined self; and the need for relationships. In addition to these themes, I have observed a journey from adversity to altruism that can be seen in the lives of those who have come through difficulty well, a journey in which healing takes place through altruistic activity. Resilience literature presented challenges to Christianity in the form of the emphasis on obedience, humility, passivity, self-denial and self-sacrifice which can inhibit the building of resilience. Issues for the resilient, to which Christian theology and pastoral practice can make a contribution, include self-reliance and difficulties with trusting others, as well as the continual struggle with self-esteem and depression to gain peace.

In turning to the Bible, it is the narratives, landscape and metaphor of the desert that resonate with the experience of adversity. The narratives of Hagar and Moses affirm the three themes that emerge in resilience literature, as well as enabling the narratives to reveal the journey from adversity to altruism expressed by pastoral responsibility. Reading the metaphor of the desert in conversation with resilience literature has enabled the discovery of three movements in the desert experience. Desert is an important biblical and spiritual theme in pastoral and spiritual literature, but it is adversity and strengthening that are emphasized, along with the experience of being solitary, not the growth or movement towards a strengthening that leads to altruism and pastoral responsibility which I have shown in the biblical and desert texts. A re-engagement with the contemporary scholarship on the historical texts of the desert reveals that it is the desert, as metaphor, that is used to inspire an embracing of adversity through the vocation to a life of asceticism. The ascetic life was lived out in many contexts in the early Christian world, not just in the desert; but it was the desert which inspired it, and still inspires Christians today. Along with Williams's reinterpretation of the tradition, contemporary life and spirituality, this readjustment of our understanding of the monastic life of the desert provides a fresh perspective on issues that were problematic, such as the place of relationships and being solitary for growth, as well as Christian understandings of the body and self-denial.

I have argued that the metaphor of the desert structures the experience of being strengthened in adversity in three movements: embracing the desert; the encounter with the self and God so as to strengthen; and the expression of altruism through which healing takes place, bringing with it pastoral responsibility. There is a broad emphasis in each movement on the resilience themes: struggle, self and relationships respectively.

The first movement of the desert metaphor – that of embracing the desert – is affirmed by resilience literature. Engaging with struggle, being motivated and open to change and growth, are necessary to come through adversity and be strengthened. The ability to acknowledge and withstand emotional pain is necessary. Embracing the desert is what Hagar, Moses and the early desert Christians did by fleeing, and they found the desert to be both a refuge and a place of adversity. The importance of attending to relationships, as well as being solitary, comes through both in resilience literature and in the monastic tradition.

The second movement of the desert metaphor – encountering the self and being strengthened by God – is a natural progression from finding oneself in the desert and being prepared to engage with it. Survival in a desert landscape requires attention to the self, involving believing oneself to have a future and facing up to the realities of the circumstances. Encounters with God in the desert, as seen through the narratives of Hagar and Moses, involve affirmation and autonomy, promise and call. They involve a continuing struggle, not release or liberation, and this requires perseverance and self-discipline.

Self-discipline is a prominent theme in the monastic life, expressed through asceticism. As I have shown, ascetical practices, like the landscape of the desert, drive people inward so that they give attention to themselves and can fight against the thought patterns that lead to vice and sin. Guarding the inner life, by staying in the cell, being resourced by prayer and Scripture, in order to fight demons, is a priority for holiness. Christian theology provides a vision for the future: the kingdom of God on earth, and life with God beyond death. As he reinterprets the monastic tradition for contemporary Christians, Rowan Williams makes it clear that self-denial is letting go of one's own perspective and creating space for another, not self-abasement. He points to the importance of autonomy for human beings as creatures, rejects passivity and calls for a deepening of pain after the pattern of Christ for growth. That said, human dependence on God and obedience remain significant, but with voice coming before silence and trust before obedience.

For the third movement of the desert metaphor, expressed through altruistic activity and pastoral responsibility, I have explored the Greek myth of the wounded healer and the psychological literature that has been used by pastoral theologians to make sense of the way in which caring for others is costly and yet brings about healing. The process reflects the pattern of Christ, who heals humanity by both descending into the depths of death and hell and rising to new life. Christ's resurrection life is what brings about healing. For Jesus, knowing he was beloved of God, having a circle of disciples, choosing to take up the cup, and then letting go in trust and obedience are what enabled the shift from death to life to take place. Here we see the features of resilient living in themes of struggle, self and relationships.

The pastoral theology of resilience that I have forged shows that adversity and strengthening are part of the life we live as creatures and are the way in which we grow and mature as human beings and Christian disciples. This is as true for pastors as they care for others as for anyone else. Resilient pastors are those who grow and mature through the costliness of altruism and pastoral responsibility, and in doing so can bring about healing.

Since the desert experience is portrayed in many different ways – through biblical stories, metaphorical use in the Bible and the landscape itself, as well as in the many texts that come out of the desert or draw on desert spirituality – it is not prescriptive of a process. Indeed, experiences of adversity recur throughout life, large and small, and the metaphor can speak at many levels and into different situations. Viewing adversity through the desert metaphor outlines the challenge that struggle, trauma, illness or bereavement brings. It offers hope for a future beyond this first stage, through honesty and encounter with the self and God in a way that strengthens, and then an invitation to come through and, in doing so, give something back while discovering further strengthening and healing.

## HELPING PEOPLE IN ADVERSITY TO BE STRENGTHENED: IMPLICATIONS FOR TEACHING AND PASTORAL CARE

The vividness of the images and themes of the desert resonate with people's experience and so the process and dynamics of resilience can be understood or remembered even by those in shock or pain, and the three movements provide a path on which to travel. Indeed, the use of metaphor and popular concepts here – desert and resilience – as well as the easily understood themes of struggle, self and relationships, along with wounded healer, speech and space, provide a rich resource for ordinary people in adversity. The obvious implication for teaching and preaching is to present these images and themes in such a way as to build resilience rather than undermine it. Adversity is not unusual. It is part of human life, and one of the tasks of Christian preaching and teaching is to enable people to be strengthened in the adversity they are experiencing in the present, prepare for adversity in the future, and find healing from the adversity of the past.

There are numerous opportunities to explore the desert as adversity, and to move on to teach that embracing the desert by being aware of one's situation, willing to struggle and open to change is also an opportunity to encounter God and be strengthened. The story does not end there, however, but leads to an empathy and compassion that is expressed in altruism, and a future. Not only in the stories of Hagar and Moses that I have chosen to explore, but also in the journey of the children of Israel through the desert, the stories of Elijah, John the Baptist and Jesus in the wilderness, to cite but a few, we find these themes. The seasons of Advent and Lent in particular provide opportunities to teach Christians how they may encourage one another to come through difficulty well, stronger in faith, hope and love.

Many Christian pastors, of course, work with people who do not espouse Christian faith. Using the biblical metaphor of the desert, which is also prevalent in other faith traditions, means that I hope what I have explored will resource Christian pastors, chaplains and those conducting funerals for congregations unfamiliar with Christian theology to nourish those in adversity so that they might be strengthened by the resonances of the desert metaphor, and by the grace of God.

Strengthening through adversity is a *process*. Growing, maturing and healing are not things that happen overnight. Helping people to understand this and thus not to panic or fear for others in a dark place would do much to help Christians support one another effectively. Recognizing the importance of being alone and staying in your cell or sitting with your stuff, as well as relating to others in a way that respects autonomy and choice and is mutual, can be seen in the experiences of the biblical characters already mentioned. Pastors always have to work against the human inclination to resist self-awareness, and the pride that means that we would rather not acknowledge the difficulties and struggles of life. Preaching and teaching that emphasizes the process of growth in Christian discipleship points to the importance of openness to change, resisting any sense of a static or passive self being a virtue.

The seasons of Advent and Lent, along with any teaching on the practice of prayer, are gifts when it comes to exploring the importance of a resourced and disciplined self. In recent years, there seems to have been a shift from giving things up for Lent to taking something on. Both are necessary to develop a resourced and disciplined inner life. To prepare to come through adversity well a person needs to have a resourced inner life, which a particular discipline of prayer encouraged every year and a traditional Lent course or group can go some way to provide. Self-discipline is vital and pastors would do well to explore with their congregations the dynamics of why this is the case and link it to other common practices such as exercise and diet. I have always been bemused as to why the practice of fasting is so little observed in churches, while detoxing and giving things up for Lent are so popular outside them. Now might well be the time to renew the practice of fasting, with acknowledgement of the importance of relaxation and discipline as well as the needs of the body and spirit in discerning the aims of an individual's practice.

Teaching, preaching and the recommendation of spiritual and prayerful practices, such as quiet days and retreats, can help prepare people to face adversity. The pastoral care offered to people experiencing adversity, whether at the church door, on the street or during a more formal visit, should acknowledge and support the motivation to struggle. The struggle to survive and attain a better quality of life needs to be honoured and encouraged so that people can embrace the desert of adversity and begin the journey of being strengthened through it. Passivity and self-abasement need to be discouraged and affirmation and autonomy brought to the fore to enable people to have the motivation to struggle and the self-esteem and vision of the future necessary for survival and strengthening.

Resilience is built by healthy, supportive and mutual relationships. Careful consideration needs to be given in teaching, preaching and one-to-one advice so that people can discern when to embrace the desert and flee – when in difficult or abusive relationships – or embrace the desert and endure, working towards a better quality of life. Subtlety is required in teaching about humility, self-denial and self-sacrifice, for these are virtues that are to be expressed from a position of knowing oneself to be significant and desired by God, and able to make space for another. Obedience is not a submission to a command, but a conscious placing of trust in God or a guide, who can enable the difficult journey of deepening pain in order to heal and free someone from the tyranny of an oppressive autonomy. All this needs to be in the context of encouraging a faith that is open to growth, aware of the riskiness of human relating and resourced by the Christian vision.

Self-awareness means that people become aware of their qualities and strengths as well as their weaknesses and sins. Remorse needs to be recognized and sin acknowledged. For many some sort of formal hearing of their confession, recognition of their sorrow and knowledge that God forgives and heals is required. This can be difficult for pastors to discern and respond to appropriately unless they are priests familiar with the practice and dynamics of the Sacrament of Reconciliation. Knowing your sins are forgiven is a vital part of being able to let go of the past and move forward as a person, relating to others in a way that means you can both give and receive. This relates, of course, to the place of forgiving others in the life of the Christian.

Pastors need to take care that their first response to someone in adversity and harmed by someone else is to help him or her to gain the strength needed to face the situation and make whatever changes are necessary, helped by others and by God. The 3 Cs of resilience are *Coping*, *Constancy*, that is, resisting destruction, and *Constructing*, that is, reconstructing one's life and sense of self. This is what someone harmed by another needs to develop in order to come through well. Christian pastors can much too quickly and inappropriately focus on forgiveness, rather than on justice or healing. This places the focus on the perpetrator, which when premature impedes both healing and the ability to offer forgiveness. Pastors would do well to draw on the three stages of the desert metaphor which enables resilience. Let us take the example of a girl or woman who has been sinned against, abused perhaps, by someone who should have protected her such as a parent or partner. She might find it difficult to acknowledge that sin and the situation she finds herself in, not wanting to believe it, thinking it might change. Embracing this desert adversity comes first in the process of resilience. It may well involve flight to a place of safety as well as recognizing that what is going on is wrong. In encountering herself the woman can acknowledge the limitations and possibilities in her life, her own strengths, worth, priorities, need for healing and what God wants for her life. For the pastor, enabling someone to encounter the self and God involves helping her to know she is valuable, loved by God, and can come through. This may well be difficult for someone who has found it hard to distinguish between love and abuse in her most intimate relationships. The sense of self, of having worth, is the basis of entering the third stage of altruism and pastoral responsibility: here, on the path of building resilience, the woman will look at how to relate to the person who hurt her. Forging a relationship where truth is acknowledged may be possible and the issue of forgiveness will emerge. Of course there may be no possibility of reconciliation, due to death or the needs of safety. To present forgiveness as the first step does not enable resilience.

There are obvious wider implications for the conversation between pastoral theology and resilience literature. A major area of the work of the churches is supporting people at particular turning points in life, particularly births, marriages and deaths, and resilience research affirms the importance of appropriate intervention at such changes in people's lives. We know that protection and nurturing are essential to resilience, and this highlights the importance of good practice in conveying values and beliefs in churches as well as in promoting a Christian lifestyle practically in interactions and dynamics in congregations and groups. The importance of 'surrogate' relationships for children and teenagers challenges the extremes of the current emphasis on protecting children from abusive relationships so that children and adults can be discouraged from forming relationships at all. Churches can be places that provide safe physical environments and people for troubled children and teenagers to form relationships with. There will be adults who can inspire and mentor – people we know who could enable those struggling to build resilience.

Pastors, especially clergy, are those who oversee, formally or informally, other pastors. The wounded-healer myths and model provide explanations of why people might be drawn to pastoral ministry and why that ministry can be personally costly to the pastor. This has implications for the selection, training and formation of pastors, ordained and lay, primarily that they be guided or supervised by others who have 'been there', and can understand the dynamics of healing in their own lives.

## THE RESILIENT PASTOR

The pastoral theology of resilience that I am forging is not a handbook of hints and tips to help pastors help others. It's a process of growing in maturity, wisdom and compassion, which emerges in those who have experienced adversity and come through it well – a process for the pastor as much as those in his or her care.

What I have offered, I hope, is a rich resource to nourish the faith and understanding of pastors regarding the process of growing, healing and being strengthened as Christian disciples. The use of a metaphor with three movements makes explicit a vocational journey for the pastor. It can enable a self-awareness and critique with regard to the practice of pastoral ministry, and one that does not leave the pastor in woundedness, but explains a process and commends a discipline which will strengthen both the pastor and his or her ministry. It also provides a challenge, that those in the pastor's care should actually find strength, hope and healing. By making explicit the processes of resilience the metaphor can challenge any theological assumptions of what is going on for the pastor and in the pastoral relationship, and so promote reflection and better practice.

Resilience literature hints at a journey from adversity to altruism and begins to explore the dynamics of how healing can be found through helping others. Although altruism is not the word Christian pastors generally use to describe their ministry, any ministry that is not altruistic can hardly be described as pastoral care. The narratives of Hagar and Moses point to adversity bringing about empathy and leading to pastoral responsibility. The Moses narrative outlines the importance of having been through the desert experience in order to lead others through it. Altruism is an important aspect of the monastic life, shown by hospitality and almsgiving and particularly in the relationship between elder and disciple. This pastoral theology of resilience seeks to invite pastors beyond a knowledge of the dynamics of pastoral care, beyond the teaching of the faith, to following something of what the desert mothers and fathers can teach us by the way in which they lived. These elders are described as healers rather than teachers, and their authority comes from their experience of the struggle to grow in holiness and their humility. They show the way for disciples to grow, listen to the manifestation of thoughts and discern what is best for the disciples. Their disciples had to be humble enough to learn and had to obey the elder. No one expects the relationship between a pastor and a member of the congregation to involve obedience in the way that the desert elders did. To be mindful of the power and authority of pastors in congregations, however, would reveal that what we say is very often heard and taken in. Those who seek particular pastors out do so because they trust them and, especially when they are vulnerable and facing difficulty, that trust means that advice is followed. Thus pastors must take care of what they say so that their words, in the context of an individual's situation, lead to life.

Obviously, it is the psychological literature around the myth and model of the wounded healer that has been very influential in exploring the dynamics of healing and growth in a pastoral relationship. Here we can find an explanation of how pastors who are aware of their own woundedness and have come through adversity can in a relationship of mutuality create the space for others to find healing. Enriched by Williams's theology, we can see that by practising detachment and yet also being involved the pastor enters into a wounded-healer relationship in which both are healed. The relationship is demanding for the pastor and requires discernment. When a pastor affirms the importance of struggling with the purpose of finding a cure or solution, it is possible for someone to gain trust and so be helped to let go when it is a shift from struggle to letting go that is necessary. Embracing that desert will drive the person inward so that an inner shift can take place in the depths of that person – the place where God may be found. Such a shift means trusting in those who care and letting go of the self. Where a person is dying, this denotes an acceptance of what is happening and of the fact that healing will not be cure, but death. Thus the language of trust, which might be described as obedience to the advice of the pastor, of letting go, and even of surrender, has its place. Such language, however, is not a substitute for struggle, an open, resourced and disciplined self or working towards appropriate relationships – rather it is the result of these. What are needed in the pastor are humility and a commitment to mutuality.

Pastors, especially clergy, have to deal with the trappings of status and authority, which do not lend themselves to many relationships of mutuality. It is vital that clergy, in particular, pursue and maintain friendships in which they can be cherished and challenged as people, regardless of other roles. Regular visits to a spiritual director and/or supervisor can enable pastors to maintain discipline in prayer, inner resourcing by Scripture and Christian literature, and self-awareness. These things are necessary for growth in resilience – the taking up of the struggle represented by self-discipline, an open and resourced self and healthy relating.

The desert mothers and fathers, in their pithy sayings, do not speak much about prayer. Neither have I, for to address the subject in any depth would require more words than this book has space for. The prayer life of a resilient pastor, like that of any Christian disciple, requires Scripture reading, praise and intercession. All that I have said so far in this book points to the importance of the body and silence. Attention to the body, to tension and pain can enable pastors, in prayer, to understand what is going on for them. Such self-awareness can enable the pastor to be aware of the state of heart and mind of another. Sitting in silence in the presence of God allows feelings to rise which, once acknowledged, provide understanding and insight. The vice of the pastor is acedia. It is a lack of self-care, lack of attention to growth and struggle and the discipline involved in doing so. Afflicted by this vice, the pastor falls asleep, and so is lazy or throws him- or herself into busyness, often expressed in taking on other people's problems. Both extremes fail to reach those who need a good pastor to discern what is needful for their situation. A resilient pastor will be familiar with the struggle to be disciplined in the kind of prayer that exposes all to God, as well as the encounter with the self and God, from which grow compassion, wisdom and strength, a contemplation which brings healing.

## Questions for reflection

1  What has been significant in helping you be strengthened by adversity over the course of your life? You might think through the three stages of embracing the desert, encountering the self and God and developing altruism or pastoral responsibility.

2  How have you experienced the vice of acedia? How might an understanding of the processes of resilience counteract it?

3  How has your experience of adversity impacted on your discipleship and ministry?

4  What adjustments need to be made in the preaching, teaching and pastoral ministry of your local congregation to acknowledge the importance of struggle, self-esteem and healthy relationships?

5  How could pastors be better selected, trained, supported and supervised?

6  In what ways might you be described as a resilient pastor or a wounded healer? How might you build resilience?

# Notes

## 1 The need for resilience in pastoral ministry

1   Osmer, R. 2008. *Practical Theology: An Introduction*, Grand Rapids, Eerdmans, p. 19.
2   Pattison, S. 2000. *A Critique of Pastoral Care*, London, SCM Press, pp. 230–4; Woodward, J. and Pattison, S. 2000. *The Blackwell Reader in Pastoral and Practical Theology*, Oxford, Blackwell, p. 139.
3   Francis, L. J. and Richter, P. 2007. *Gone for Good?: Church – Leaving and Returning in the 21st Century*, Peterborough, Epworth, pp, 222–4.
4   Leach, J. and Paterson, M. 2010. *Pastoral Supervision: A Handbook*, London, SCM Press; Ward, F. 2005. *Lifelong Learning: Theological Education and Supervision*, London, SCM Press.
5   Ward, *Lifelong Learning*.
6   Lane, B. C. 1998. *The Solace of Fierce Landscapes: Exploring Desert and Mountain Spirituality*, Oxford, Oxford University Press; Nouwen, H. J. M. 1981. *Way of the Heart: Desert Spirituality and Contemporary Ministry*, New York, Seabury Press; Moody, C. 1992. *Eccentric Ministry: Pastoral Care and Leadership in the Parish*, London, Darton, Longman & Todd.

## 2 Developing resilience: research and themes

1   Werner, E. E. and Smith, R. S. 1982. *Vulnerable but Invincible: A Longitudinal Study of Resilient Children and Youth*, New York and London, McGraw-Hill; Werner, E. E. and Smith, R. S. 1992. *Overcoming the Odds: High Risk Children from Birth to Adulthood*, Ithaca and London, Cornell University Press.
2   Rutter, M. 1985. 'Resilience in the Face of Adversity: Protective Factors and Resistance to Psychiatric Disorder', *British Journal of Psychiatry*, 598–611; Rutter, M. et al. 1998. 'Developmental Catch-up

and Deficit, Following Adoption after Severe Global Early Privation', *Journal of Child Psychology and Psychiatry*, 465–76.

3 Titus, C. S. 2006. *Resilience and the Virtue of Fortitude: Aquinas in Dialogue with the Psychosocial Sciences*, Washington, DC, Catholic University of America Press.

4 The four cardinal virtues are justice, prudence, temperance and fortitude.

5 Frankl, V. E. and Frankl, V. E. F. D.-C. T. E. 2004. *Man's Search for Meaning: The Classic Tribute to Hope from the Holocaust*, London, Rider, p. 74.

6 Frankl and Frankl, *Man's Search for Meaning*, p. 49.

7 Higgins, G. O'C. 1994. *Resilient Adults: Overcoming a Cruel Past*, San Francisco, Jossey-Bass, ch. 7.

8 Higgins, *Resilient Adults*.

9 Wolin, S. J. and Wolin, S. 1993. *The Resilient Self: How Survivors of Troubled Families Rise Above Adversity*, New York, Villard Books.

10 Tangney, J. P. 2000. 'Humility: Theoretical Perspectives, Empirical Findings and Directions for Future Research', *Journal of Social and Clinical Psychology*, 19, 73–4.

11 Higgins, *Resilient Adults*, pp. 192–8.

## 3 The desert: landscape and metaphor for developing resilience

1 Trible, P. 1984. *Texts of Terror: Literary-feminist Readings of Biblical Narratives*, Philadelphia, Fortress Press, pp. 27–8.

2 Williams, D. 2006. 'Hagar in African American Biblical Appropriation' in Trible, P. and Letty, M. (eds), *Hagar, Sarah, and Their Children: Jewish, Christian and Muslim Perspectives*, Louisville, KY, Westminster John Knox, p. 177.

3 Hassan, R. 2006. 'Islamic Hagar and Her Family' in Trible, *Hagar, Sarah, and Their Children*, p. 155.

4 Haddad, Y. Y. and Esposito, J. L. 2001. *Daughters of Abraham: Feminist Thought in Judaism, Christianity and Islam*, Gainesville, University Press of Florida, pp. 81–6.

5 Jasper, D. 2004. *The Sacred Desert: Religion, Literature, Art and Culture*, Oxford, Blackwell, p. 26.

6 Brown, P. R. L. 1982. *Society and the Holy in Late Antiquity*, Berkeley, California University Press, pp. 109–12; Brown, P. R. L. 1971. *The World of Late Antiquity: From Marcus Aurelius to Muhammad*, London, Thames and Hudson, pp. 96–112.

7  Storr, A. 1988. *Solitude*, London, Flamingo, 1989, p. 50.

## 4 Desert Christians embrace adversity for growth

1  Quotes from the *Sayings* come from the translation by Ward, B. 1975. *The Sayings of the Desert Fathers: The Alphabetical Collection*, London, Mowbray.
2  Merton, T. 1961. *The Wisdom of the Desert: Sayings from the Desert Fathers of the Fourth Century*, London, Hollis and Carter, p. 8.
3  Stewart, C. 1998. *Cassian the Monk*, New York and Oxford, Oxford University Press, pp. 40, 42, 46.
4  Stewart, C. 1990. 'Radical Honesty about the Self: The Practice of the Desert Fathers', *Sobornost*, 12, p. 26.

## 5 Rowan Williams and resilient believing

1  See the lectures he gave in 2001 for the World Community for Christian Meditation, published as *Silence and Honey Cakes: The Wisdom of the Desert* (2003, Oxford, Lion).
2  Williams, R. 2000. *Lost Icons: Reflections on Cultural Bereavement*, Harrisburg, PA and London, Morehouse, pp. 145–55.
3  Williams, R. 1983. *The Truce of God*, London, Fount, p. 76.
4  Williams, R. 1979. *The Wound of Knowledge*, London, Darton, Longman & Todd, p. 11.
5  Williams, *The Wound of Knowledge*, pp. 12–13, 59, 182.
6  Williams, *The Wound of Knowledge*, pp. 177–80.
7  Williams, R. 2000. 'On Being Creatures' in Williams, R. (ed.), *On Christian Theology*, Oxford, Blackwell, p. 72.
8  Williams, 'On Being Creatures', p. 75.
9  Williams, *Silence and Honey Cakes*, pp. 94, 98.
10 Williams, R. 2007. *Tokens of Trust: An Introduction to Christian Belief*, Norwich, Canterbury Press, p. 109.
11 Williams, R. 2007. 'A Theology of Health for Today' in Baxter, J. (ed.), *Wounds that Heal: Theology, Imagination and Health*, London, SPCK.
12 See Williams, *Lost Icons*, pp. 155–7 for the discussion of being in love.
13 Williams, R. 2004. 'The Christian Priest Today'. Lecture at Ripon College, Cuddesdon, Oxford. www.archbishopofcanterbury.org
14 See Williams, R. 1989. *Christianity and the Ideal of Detachment*, Clinical Theology Association.
15 Williams, R. 2002. *Writing in the Dust: Reflections on 11th September and Its Aftermath*, London, Hodder & Stoughton.

## 6 From wounded healer to resilient pastor

1 Nash, S. and Nash, P. 2009. *Tools for Reflective Ministry*, London, SPCK, pp. 62–4.

2 Nouwen, H. J. M. 1979. *The Wounded Healer: Ministry in Contemporary Society*, Garden City, NY, Doubleday, p. 72.

3 Campbell, A. V. 1986. *Rediscovering Pastoral Care*, London, Darton, Longman & Todd, pp. 12–15, 41–3.

4 Campbell, *Rediscovering Pastoral Care*, pp. 37–8.

5 Kearney, M. 1996. *Mortally Wounded: Stories of Soul Pain, Death and Healing*, Dublin, Marino, pp. 44–7, 159.

6 Maeder, T. 1989. *Children of Psychiatrists and Other Psychotherapists*, New York, Harper & Row, p. 37; see also Sussman, M. 1992. *Curious Calling: Unconscious Motivations for Practicing Psychotherapy*, Northvale, NJ, J. Aronson, p. 242.

7 Maeder, *Children of Psychiatrists*, pp. 77–9, 88.

# Further reading

## Resilience: general resources

Aquinas, T. (Trans. Walsh, P. G.) 2006. *Summa Theologiae*: 2a2ae. 123–40: *Courage v. 42*, Cambridge, Cambridge University Press.

Flach, F. F. 1997. *Resilience: How to Bounce Back When the Going Gets Tough!*, New York, Hatherleigh Press.

Frankl, V. E. and Frankl, V. E. F. D.-C. T. E. 2004. *Man's Search for Meaning: The Classic Tribute to Hope from the Holocaust*, London, Rider.

Graham, E. L., Walton, H. and Ward, F. 2005. *Theological Reflection: Methods*, London, SCM Press.

Graham, E. L., Walton, H. and Ward, F. 2007. *Theological Reflection: Sources*, London, SCM Press.

Higgins, G. O'C. 1994. *Resilient Adults: Overcoming a Cruel Past*, San Francisco, Jossey-Bass.

Leach, J. and Paterson, M. 2010. *Pastoral Supervision: A Handbook*, London, SCM Press.

Lifton, R. J. 1993. The *Protean Self: Human Resilience in an Age of Fragmentation*, New York, Basic Books.

Osmer, R. 2008. *Practical Theology: An Introduction*, Grand Rapids, Eerdmans.

Pattison, S. 2000. *A Critique of Pastoral Care*, London, SCM Press.

Tangney, J. P. 2000. 'Humility: Theoretical Perspectives, Empirical Findings and Directions for Future Research', *Journal of Social and Clinical Psychology*, 19, 70–82.

Ward, F. 2005. *Lifelong Learning: Theological Education and Supervision*, London, SCM Press.

Wolin, S. J. and Wolin, S. 1993. *The Resilient Self: How Survivors of Troubled Families Rise Above Adversity*, New York, Villard Books.

Woodward, J. and Pattison, S. 2000. *The Blackwell Reader in Pastoral and Practical Theology*, Oxford, Blackwell.


## The desert and desert Christians

Athanasius. (Trans. Gregg, R. C.) 1980. *The Life of Antony and the Letter to Marcellinus*, New York, Paulist Press.

Brown, P. R. L. 1971. *The World of Late Antiquity: From Marcus Aurelius to Muhammad*, London, Thames and Hudson.

Brown, P. R. L. 1982. *Society and the Holy in Late Antiquity*, Berkeley, California University Press.

Buhner, S. H. 2003. *The Fasting Path*, New York, Avery.

Carretto, C. 2002. *Letters from the Desert*, London, Darton Longman & Todd.

Cassian, J. (Trans. Ramsey, B.) 1997. *The Conferences*, New York, Newman Press.

Cassian, J. (Trans. Ramsey, B.) 2000. *The Institutes*, New York, Newman Press.

Chryssavgis, J. and Zosimas, A. F. R. E. 2003. *In the Heart of the Desert: The Spirituality of the Desert Fathers and Mothers: With a Translation of Abba Zosimas' Reflections*, Bloomington, IN, World Wisdom.

Haddad, Y. Y. and Esposito, J. L. 2001. *Daughters of Abraham: Feminist Thought in Judaism, Christianity and Islam*, Gainesville, University Press of Florida.

Jamison, C. 2008. *Finding Happiness: Monastic Steps for a Fulfilling Life*, London, Weidenfeld & Nicolson.

Jasper, D. 2004. *The Sacred Desert: Religion, Literature, Art, and Culture*, Oxford, Blackwell.

Lane, B. C. 1998. *The Solace of Fierce Landscapes: Exploring Desert and Mountain Spirituality*, Oxford, Oxford University Press.

The Makhad Trust, www.makhad.org.

Merton, T. 1961. *The Wisdom of the Desert: Sayings from the Desert Fathers of the Fourth Century*, London, Hollis and Carter.

Norris, K. 1993. *Dakota: A Spiritual Geography*, New York, Ticknor & Fields.

Norris, K. 2008. *Acedia and Me: A Marriage, Monks, and a Writer's Life*, New York, Penguin.

Ryrie, A. 2011. *The Desert Movement: Fresh Perspectives on the Spirituality of the Desert*, Norwich, Canterbury Press.

Saint-Exupéry, A. de and Rees, W. 2000. *Wind, Sand and Stars*, London, Penguin.

Solomon, A. 2002. *The Noonday Demon: An Anatomy of Depression*, London, Vintage.

Stewart, C. 1990. 'Radical Honesty about the Self: The Practice of the Desert Fathers', *Sobornost*, 12.

Stewart, C. 1998. *Cassian the Monk*, New York and Oxford, Oxford University Press.

Storr, A. 1988. *Solitude*, London, Flamingo, 1989.

Trible, P. 1984. *Texts of Terror: Literary-feminist Readings of Biblical Narratives*, Philadelphia, Fortress Press.

Trible, P. and Letty, M. (eds). 2006. *Hagar, Sarah, and Their Children: Jewish, Christian and Muslim Perspectives*, Louisville, KY, Westminster John Knox.

Ward, B. 1975. *The Sayings of the Desert Fathers: The Alphabetical Collection*, London, Mowbray.

## Rowan Williams and resilient believing

Williams, R. 1979. *The Wound of Knowledge*, London, Darton, Longman & Todd.

Williams, R. 1983. *The Truce of God*, London, Fount.

Williams, R. 1989. *Christianity and the Ideal of Detachment*, Clinical Theology Association.

Williams, R. 2000. *Lost Icons: Reflections on Cultural Bereavement*, Harrisburg, PA and London, Morehouse.

Williams, R. 2000. 'On Being Creatures'. In Williams, R. (ed.), *On Christian Theology*, Oxford, Blackwell.

Williams, R. 2002. *Writing in the Dust: Reflections on 11th September and Its Aftermath*, London, Hodder & Stoughton.

Williams, R. 2003. *Silence and Honey Cakes: The Wisdom of the Desert*, Oxford, Lion.

Williams, R. 2004. 'The Christian Priest Today'. Lecture at Ripon College, Cuddesdon, Oxford. www.archbishopofcanterbury.org.

Williams, R. 2007. 'A Theology of Health for Today' in Baxter, J. (ed.), *Wounds that Heal: Theology, Imagination and Health*, London, SPCK.

Williams, R. 2007. *Tokens of Trust: An Introduction to Christian Belief*, Norwich, Canterbury Press.

## Wounded healer and resilient pastor

Bryant, M. T. 2006. *Wounded Healers: Resilient Psychotherapists. In partial fulfilment of the requirements for the Degree Doctor of Philosophy*, Minneapolis, Capella University.

Graves, R. 1990. *The Greek Myths*, London, Penguin Books, 1960 (1990 printing).

Hockley, L. A. G. and Gardner, L. (eds). 2011. *House – The Wounded Healer on Television: Jungian and Post-Jungian Reflections*, London, Routledge.

Kearney, M. 1996. *Mortally Wounded: Stories of Soul, Pain, Death and Healing*, Dublin, Marino.

Maeder, T. 1989. *Children of Psychiatrists and Other Psychotherapists*, New York, Harper & Row.

Munroe, B. and Oliviere, D. (eds). 2007. *Resilience in Palliative Care: Achievement in Adversity*, Oxford, Oxford University Press.

Nouwen, H. J. M. 1979. *The Wounded Healer: Ministry in Contemporary Society*, Garden City, NY, Doubleday.

Sussman, M. 1992. *Curious Calling: Unconscious Motivations for Practicing Psychotherapy*, Northvale, NJ, J. Aronson.

# Index